WORSHIP SONGBOOK

Song Title	Page Number
1. Above All	2
2. As The Deer	7
3. Awesome God	9
4. Better Is One Day	13
5. Celebrate Jesus	19
6. Did You Feel The Mountains Tremble	25
7. Glorify Thy Name	31
8. God Is Good All The Time	35
9. God Will Make A Way	43
10. He Is Able	49
11. Holy And Anointed One	53
12. Holy Ground	57
13. Hungry (Falling On My Knees)	63
14. I Believe In Jesus	68
15. I See The Lord	72
16. I Walk By Faith	78
17. I Will Celebrate	83
18. I Will Not Forget You	89
19. In That Day	97
20. In The Secret	103
21. Jesus Is Alive	108
22. Jesus, Lover Of My Soul	111
23. Light The Fire Again	116
24. Redeemer, Savior, Friend	120
25. Rock Of Ages	125
26. Shine Jesus Shine	133
27. There Is None Like You	137
28. Victory Chant	142
29. We Want To See Jesus Lifted High	149
30. We Will Dance	155
31. When I Look Into Your Holiness	162
32. Worship You	165
33. You Are God	173

©2000 Integrity Incorporated
1000 Cody Road, Mobile, AL 36695-3425
All Songs Used By Permission. All Rights Reserved.
International Rights Secured.

17236

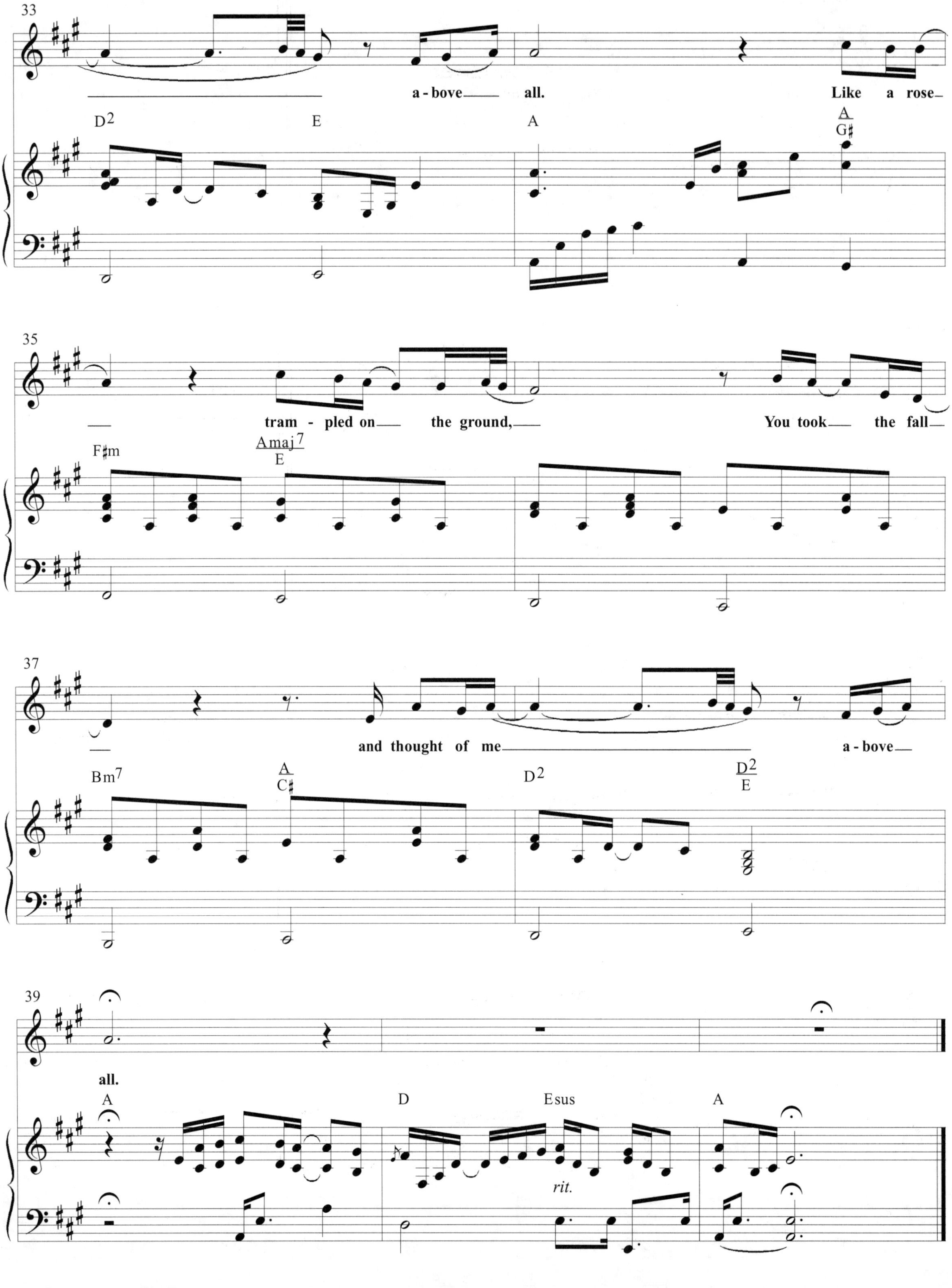
33
a - bove all.
Like a rose
D2 E A A/G♯
35
trampled on the ground,
You took the fall
F♯m Amaj7/E
37
and thought of me
a - bove
Bm7 A/C♯ D2 D2/E
39
all.
A D Esus A
rit.

As the Deer

**Words and Music by
MARTIN J. NYSTROM**

© Copyright 1984 Maranatha Praise, Inc. (administered by The Copyright Company, 40 Music Square East, Nashville, TN 37203).
All rights reserved. International copyright secured. Used by permission. CCLI# 1431

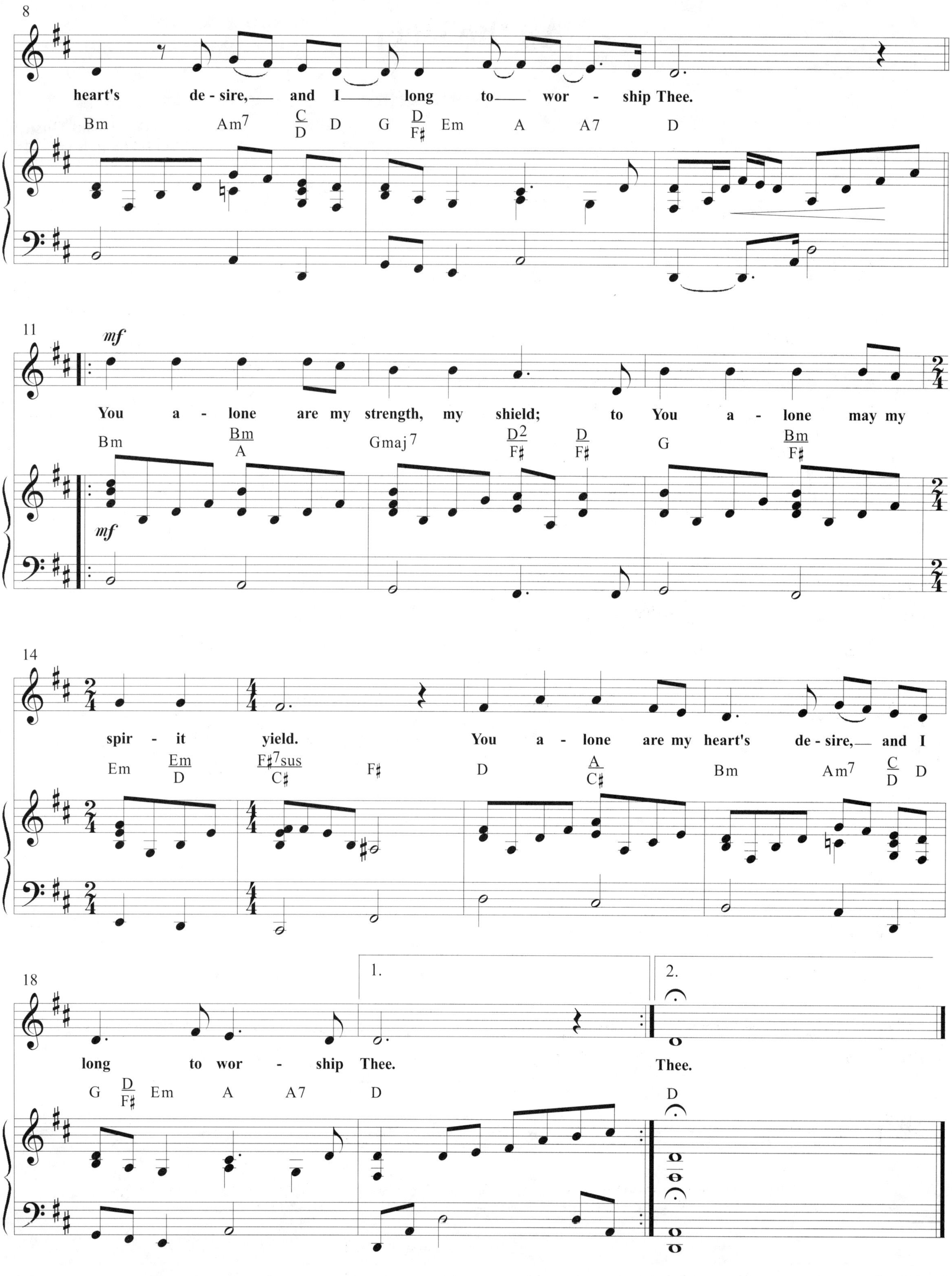
8
heart's de - sire, and I long to wor - ship Thee.
Bm Am7 C/D D G D/F♯ Em A A7 D
11
mf
You a - lone are my strength, my shield; to You a - lone may my
Bm Bm/A Gmaj7 D2/F♯ D/F♯ G Bm/F♯
mf
14
spir - it yield. You a - lone are my heart's de - sire, and I
Em Em/D F♯7sus/C♯ F♯ D A/C♯ Bm Am7 C/D D
18
1.
2.
long to wor - ship Thee. Thee.
G D/F♯ Em A A7 D D

Awesome God

Words and Music by
RICH MULLINS

© Copyright 1988 BMG Songs, Inc., 8750 Wilshire Boulevard, Beverly Hills, CA 90211.
All rights reserved. International copyright secured. Used by permission. CCLI # 41099

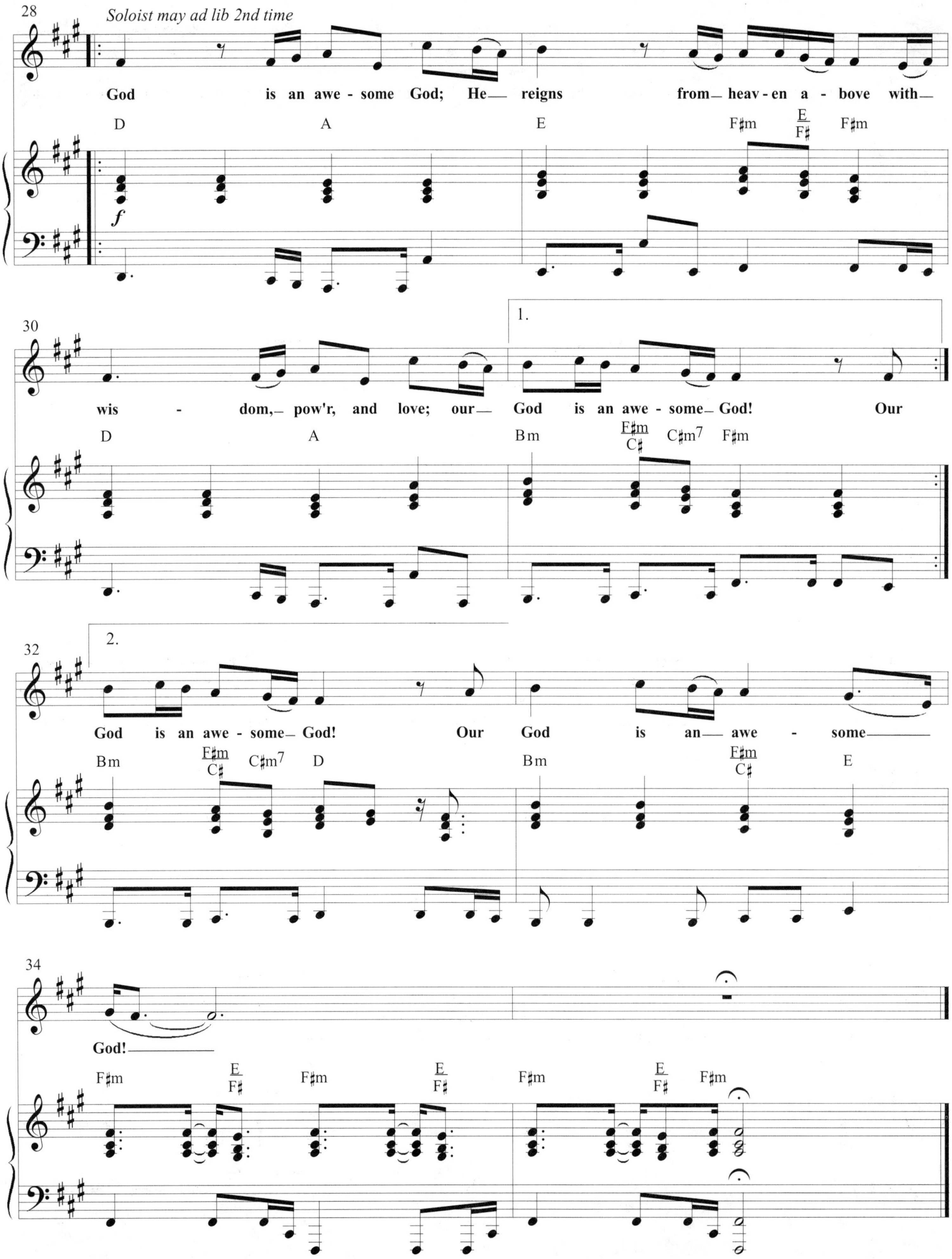
28
Soloist may ad lib 2nd time
God is an awe - some God; He reigns from heav - en a - bove with
D A E F♯m E/F♯ F♯m
f
30
wis - dom, pow'r, and love; our God is an awe - some God! Our
D A Bm F♯m/C♯ C♯m7 F♯m
1.
32
2.
God is an awe - some God! Our God is an awe - some God!
Bm F♯m/C♯ C♯m7 D Bm F♯m/C♯ E
34
F♯m E/F♯ F♯m E/F♯ F♯m E/F♯ F♯m

Better Is One Day

Words and Music by
MATT REDMAN

© Copyright 1995 Kingsway's Thankyou Music. All rights in the Western Hemisphere administered by EMI Christian Music Publishing, 101 Winners Circle, P.O. Box 5085, Brentwood, TN 37024-5085.
All rights reserved. International copyright secured. Used by permission. CCLI# 1097451

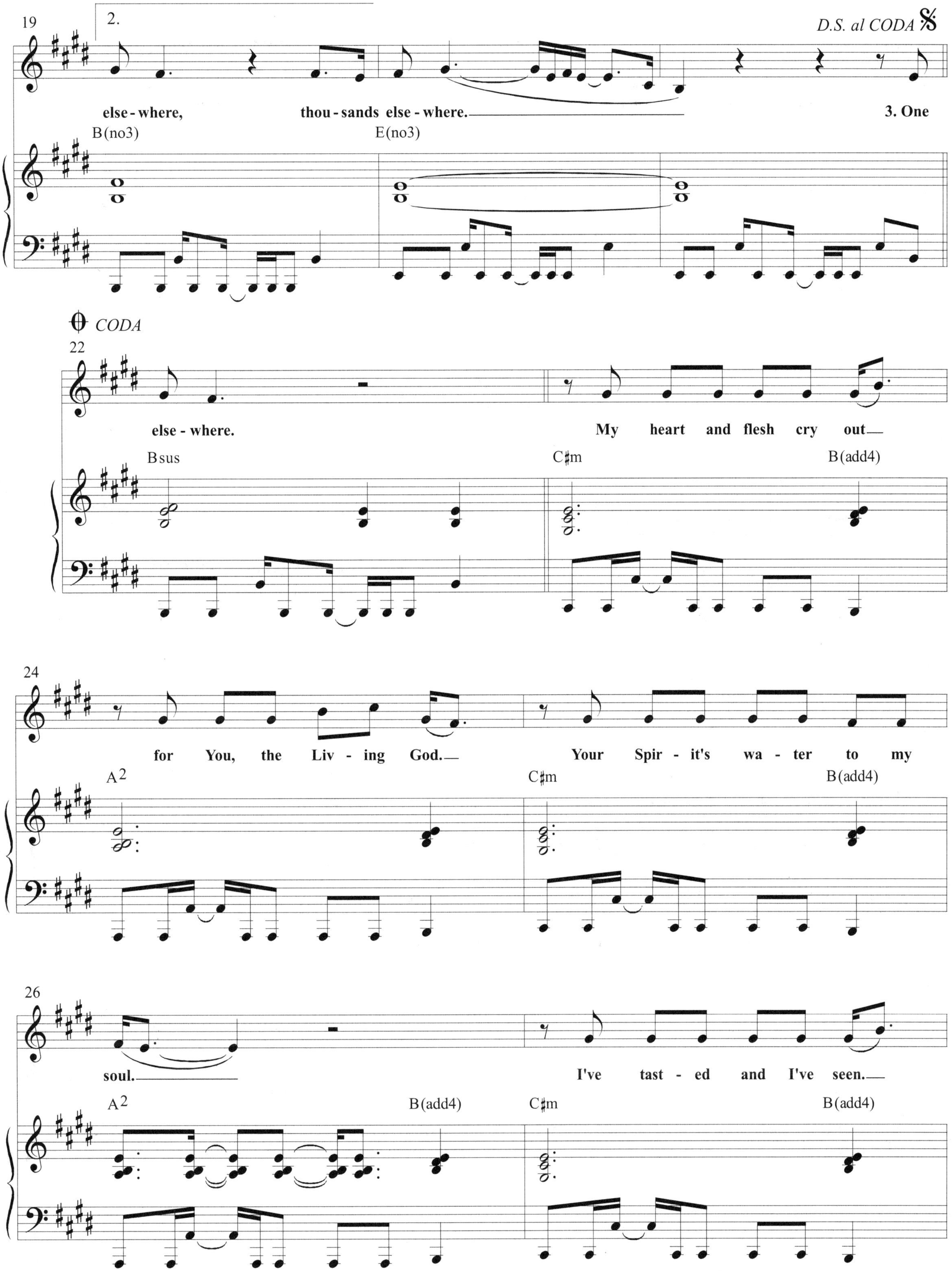
19
2.
D.S. al CODA
else - where,
thou - sands else - where.
3. One
B(no3)
E(no3)
CODA
22
else - where.
My heart and flesh cry out
Bsus
C♯m
B(add4)
24
for You, the Liv - ing God.
Your Spir - it's wa - ter to my
A2
C♯m
B(add4)
26
soul.
I've tast - ed and I've seen.
A2
B(add4)
C♯m
B(add4)

Celebrate Jesus

**Words and Music by
GARY OLIVER**

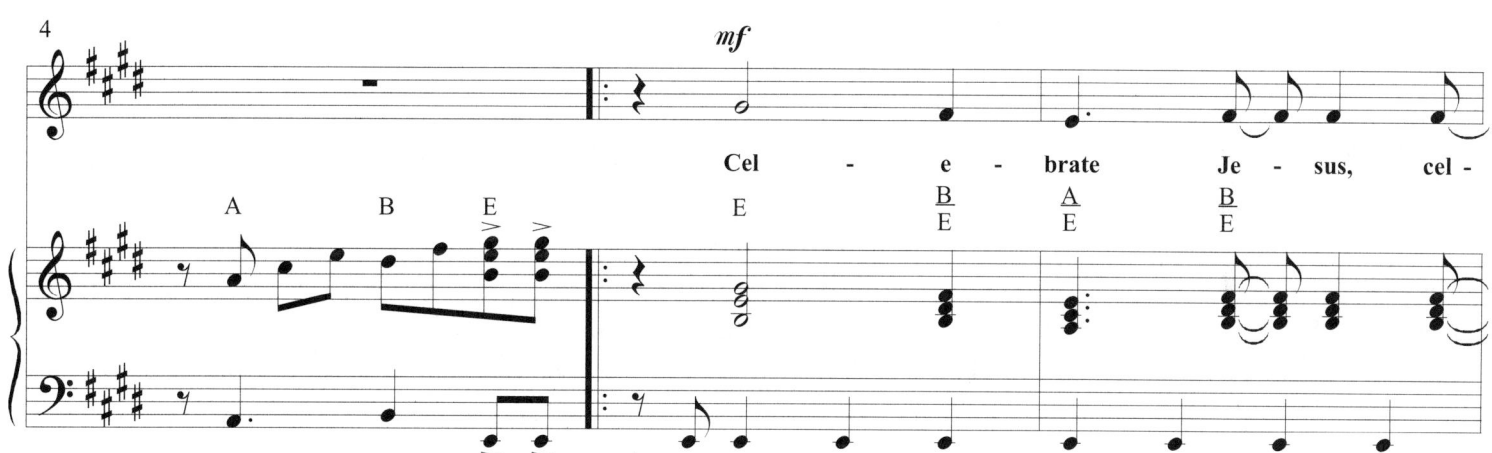

© Copyright 1988 Integrity's Hosanna! Music c/o Integrity Music, Inc., 1000 Cody Road, Mobile, AL 36695.
All rights reserved. International copyright secured. Used by permission. CCLI# 16859

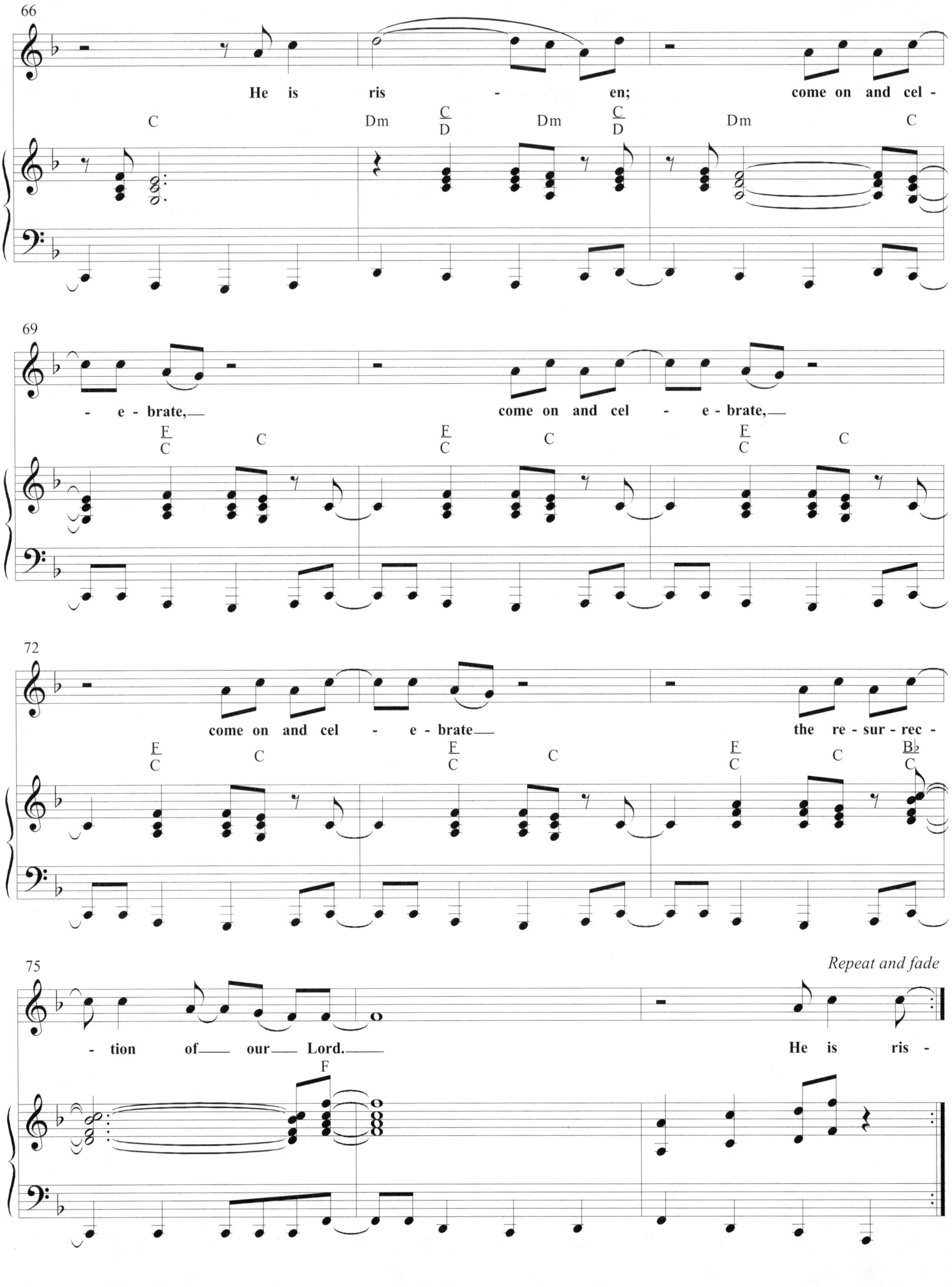
66
He is ris - en; come on and cel -
C Dm C/D Dm C/D Dm C
69
- e - brate, come on and cel - e - brate,
F/C C F/C C F/C C
72
come on and cel - e - brate the re - sur - rec -
F/C C F/C C F/C C B♭/C
75
Repeat and fade
- tion of our Lord. He is ris -
F

Did You Feel the Mountains Tremble?

Words and Music by
MARTIN SMITH

© Copyright 1994 Curious? Music UK. All rights in the United States and Canada administered by EMI Christian Music Publishing,
101 Winners Circle, P.O. Box 5085, Brentwood, TN 37204-5085.
All rights reserved. International copyright secured. Used by permission. CCLI# 1097028

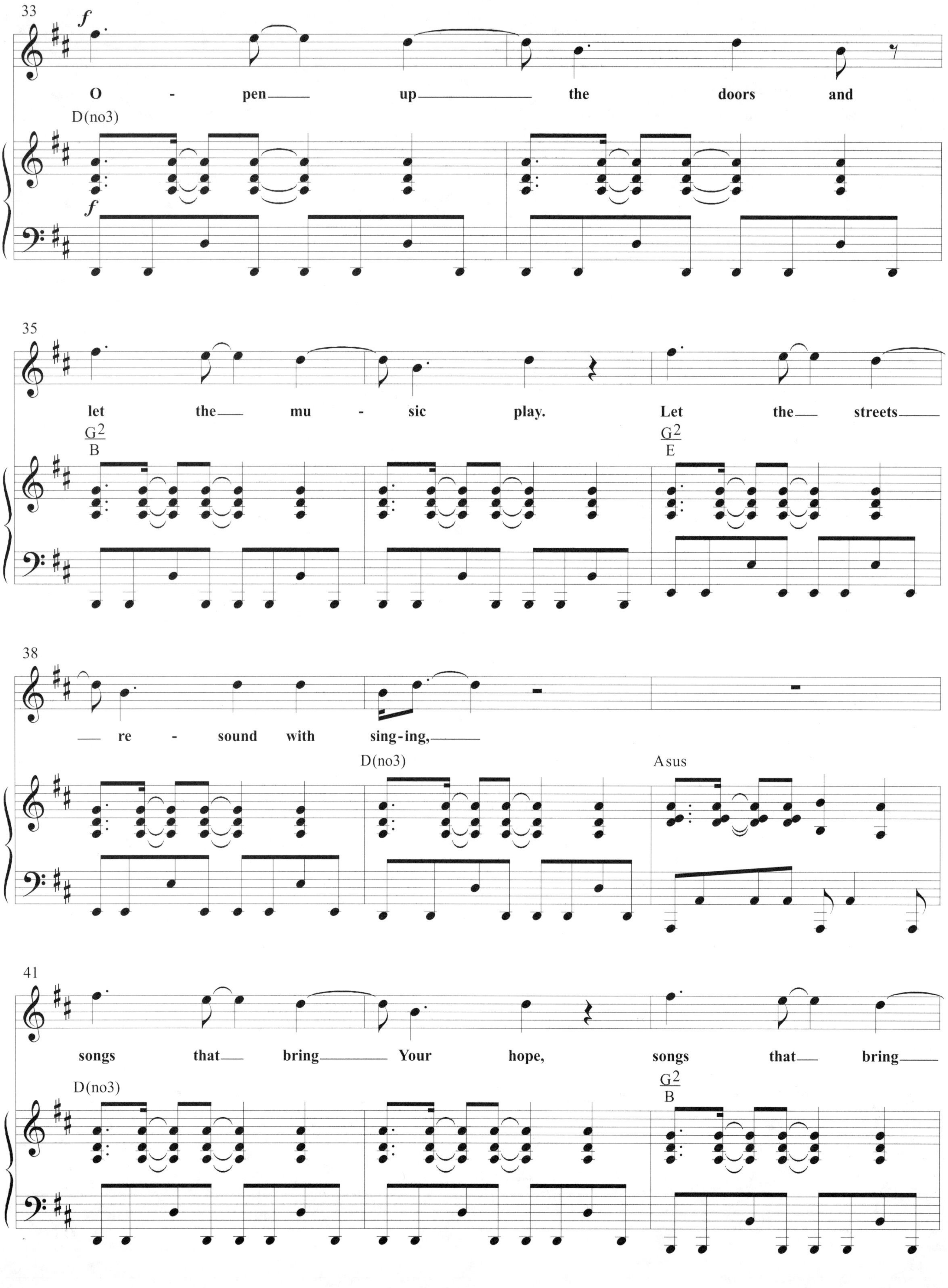
33
f
O - pen up the doors and
D(no3)
f
35
let the mu - sic play. Let the streets
G2 B
G2 E
38
re - sound with sing-ing,
D(no3)
Asus
41
songs that bring Your hope, songs that bring
D(no3)
G2 B

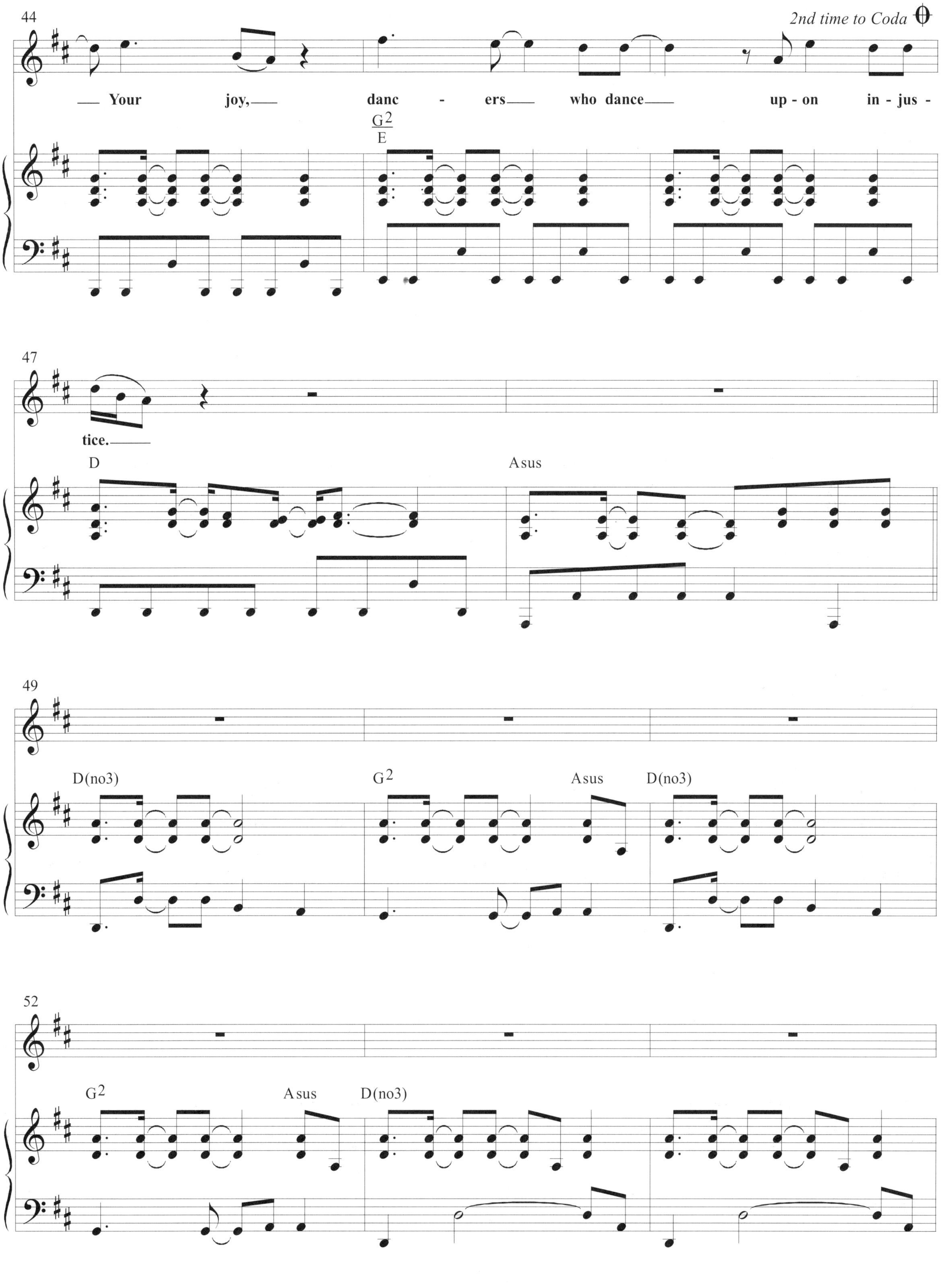
44
2nd time to Coda
Your joy, danc - ers who dance up - on in - jus -
G2/E
47
tice.
D
Asus
49
D(no3)
G2
Asus
D(no3)
52
G2
Asus
D(no3)

Glorify Thy Name

© Copyright 1976 Maranatha! Music (administered by The Copyright Company, 40 Music Square East, Nashville, TN 37203).
All rights reserved. International copyright secured. Used by permission. CCLI# 1383

God Is Good All the Time

**Words and Music by
DON MOEN and
PAUL OVERSTREET**

© Copyright 1995 Integrity's Hosanna! Music c/o Integrity Music, Inc., 1000 Cody Road, Mobile, AL 36695 and
Scarlet Moon Music c/o Copyright Management International, LLC, 1625 Broadway, 4th Floor, Nashville, TN 37203.
All rights reserved. International copyright secured. Used by permission. CCLI# 1729073

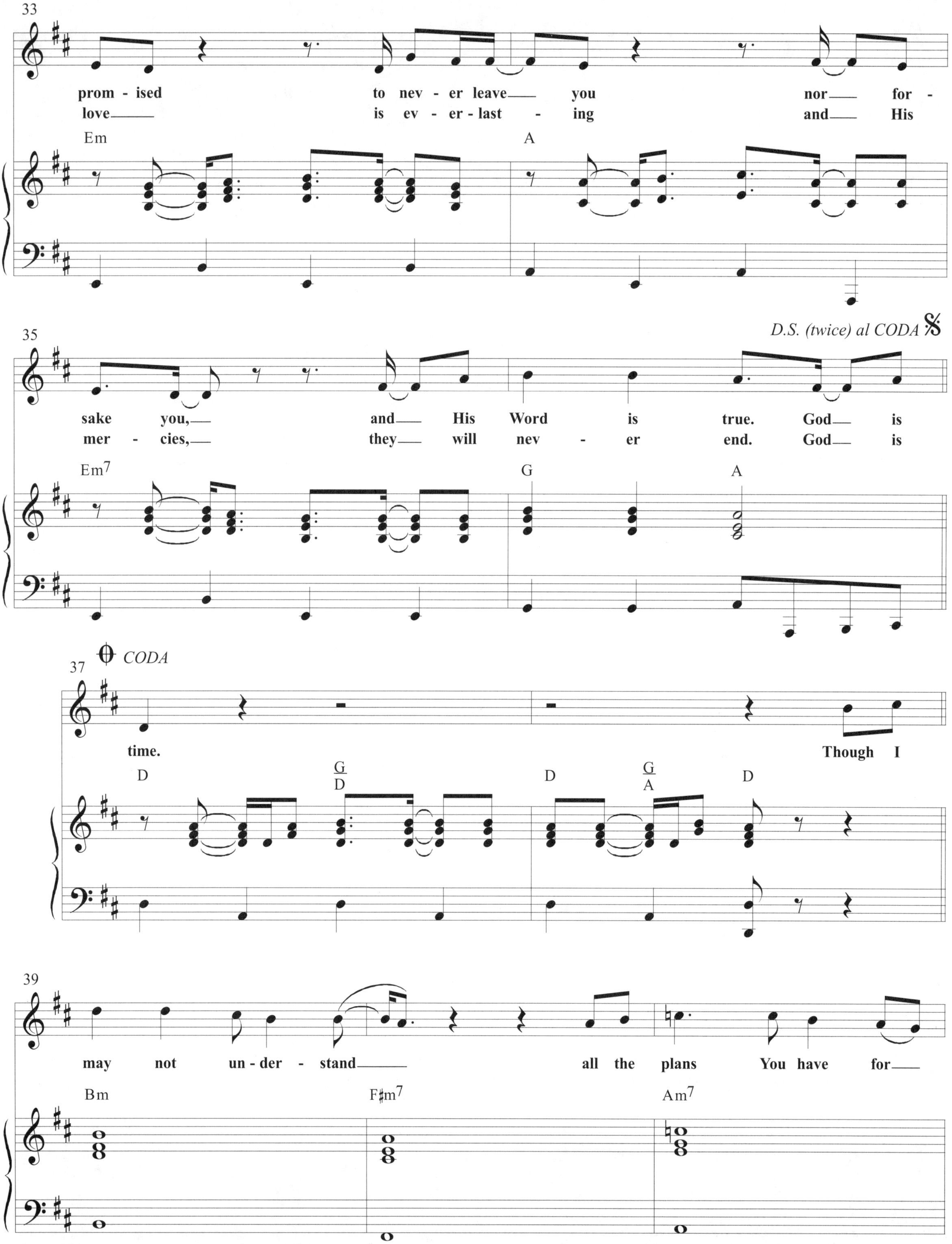
33
prom - ised to nev - er leave you nor for -
love is ev - er - last - ing and His
Em
A
35
D.S. (twice) al CODA
sake you, and His Word is true. God is
mer - cies, they will nev - er end. God is
Em7
G
A
37
CODA
time. Though I
D
G/D
D
G/A
D
39
may not un - der - stand all the plans You have for
Bm
F♯m7
Am7

good. God is good. God is good. He's good. God is good. He's so good all the time.

God Will Make a Way

**Words and Music by
DON MOEN**

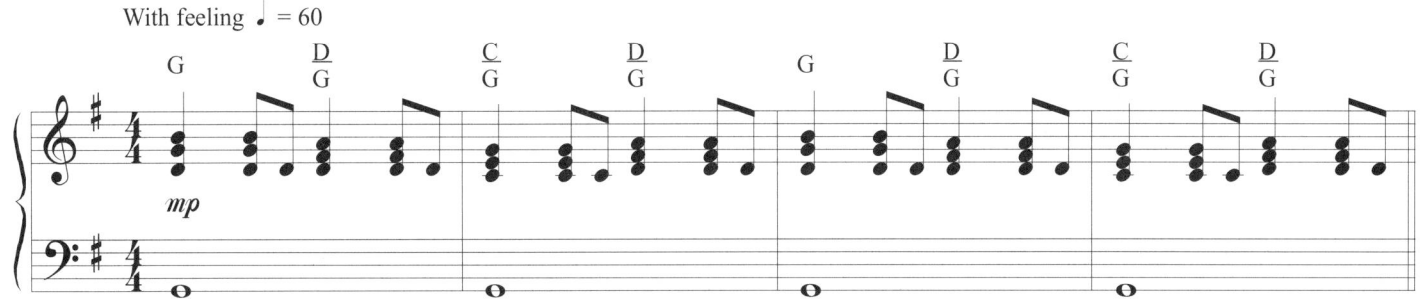

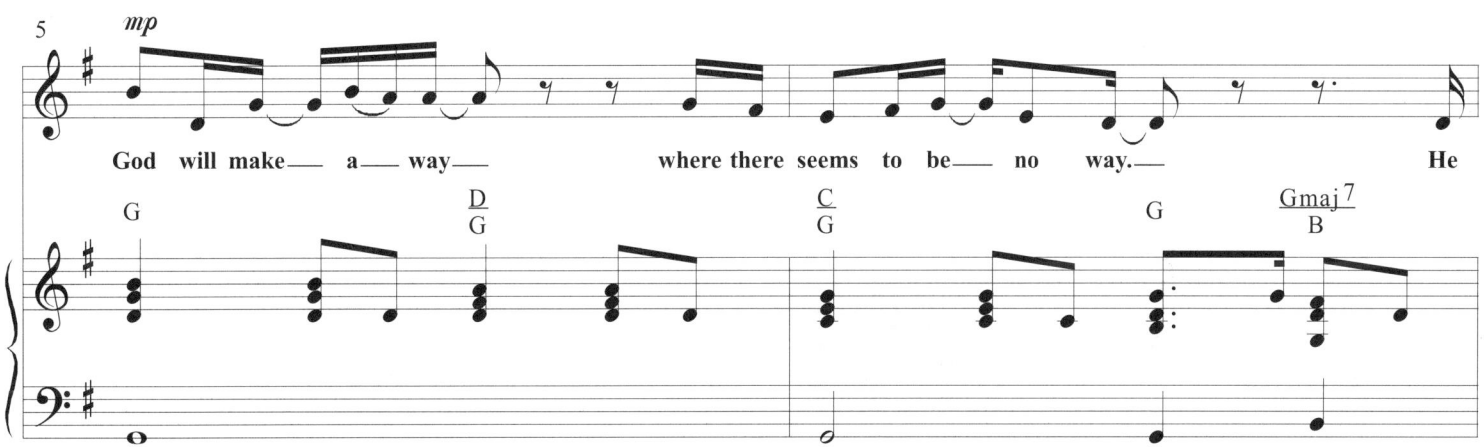

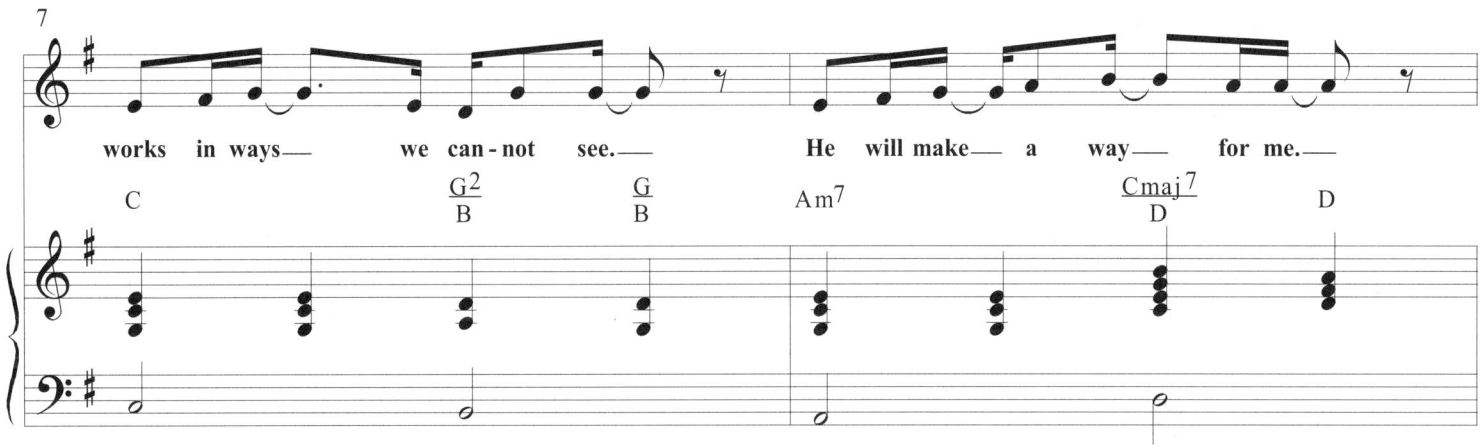

© Copyright 1990 Integrity's Hosanna! Music c/o Integrity Music, Inc., 1000 Cody Road, Mobile, AL 36695.
All rights reserved. International copyright secured. Used by permission. CCLI# 458620

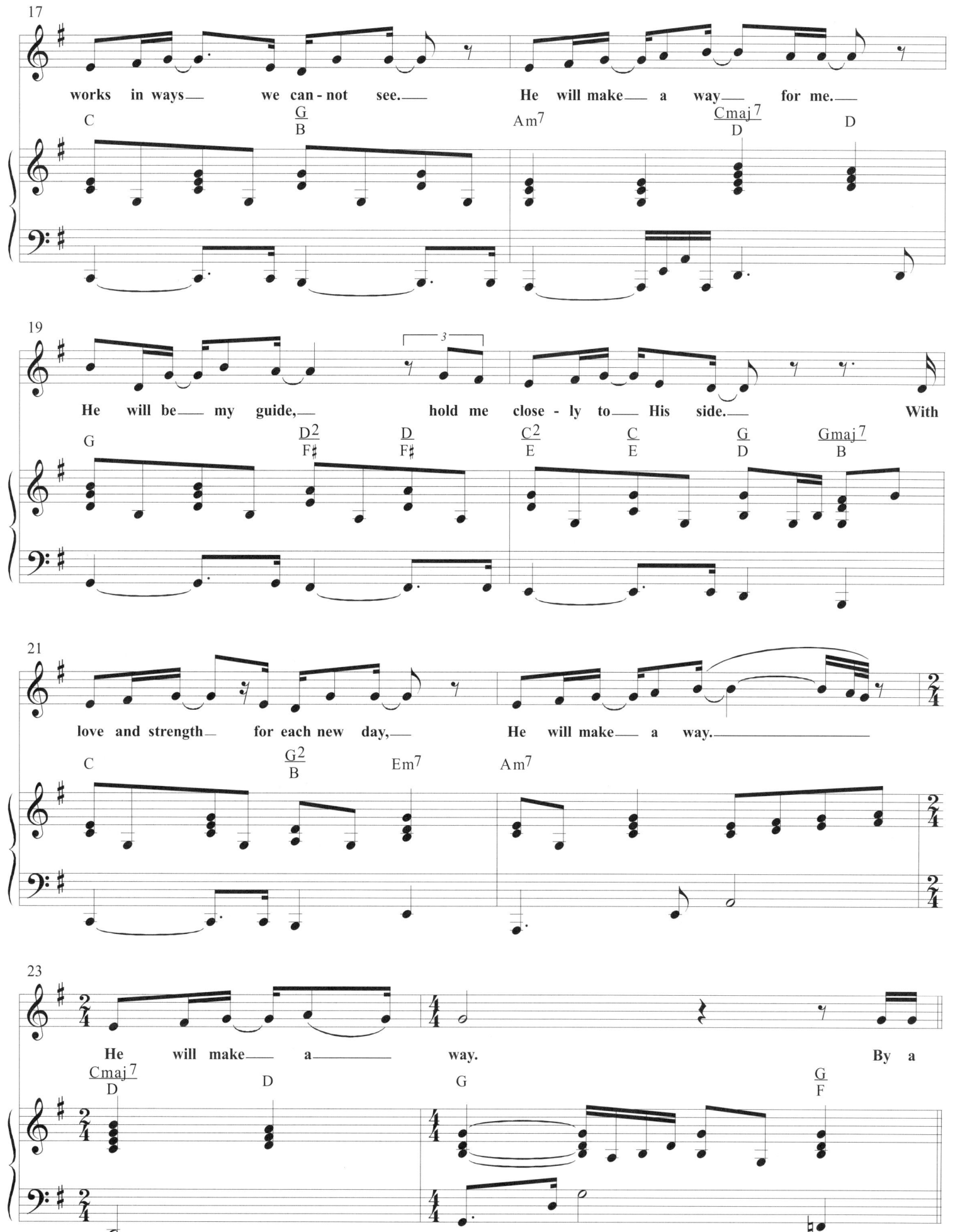

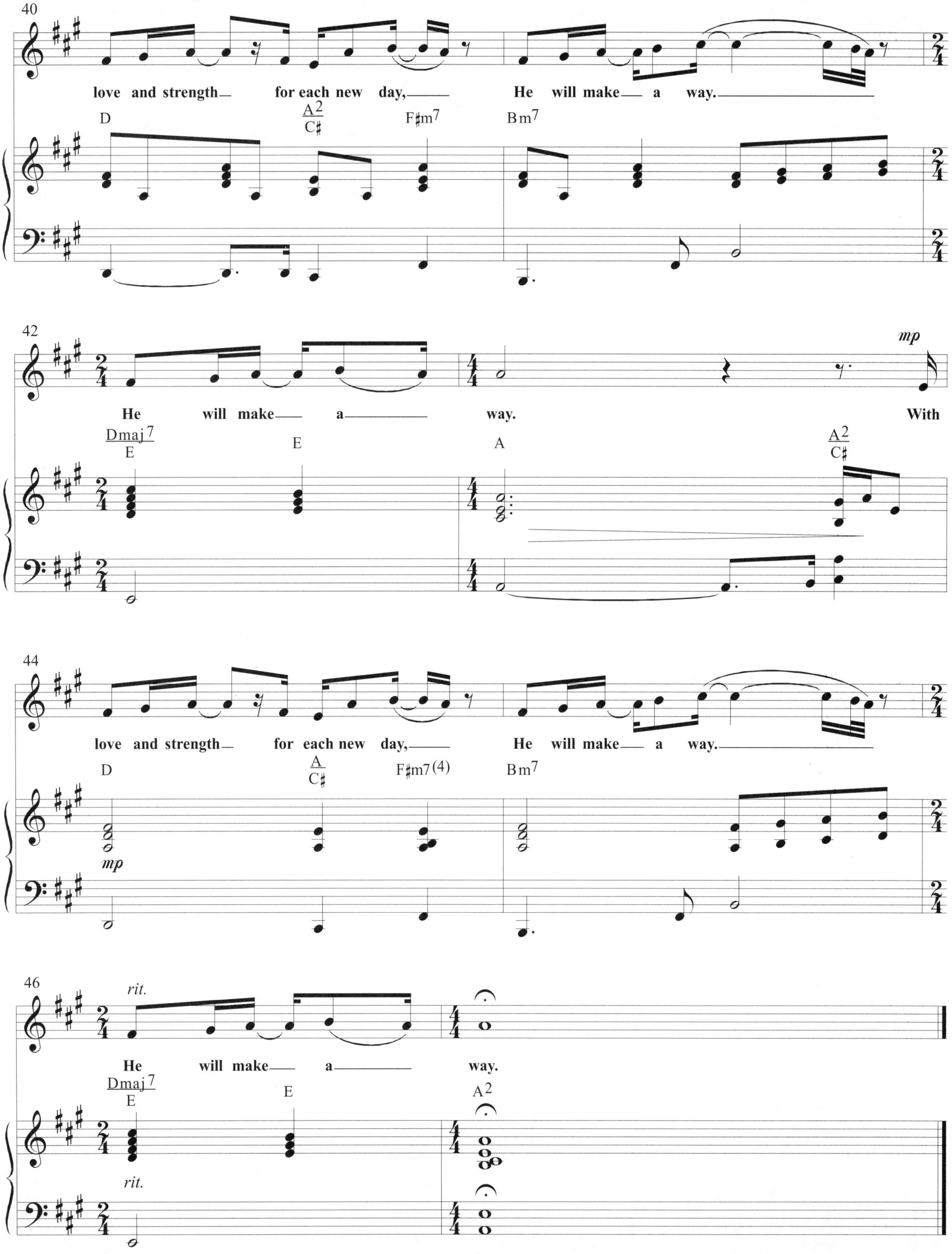
40
love and strength for each new day, He will make a way.
D
A2/C♯
F♯m7
Bm7
42
mp
He will make a way. With
Dmaj7/E
E
A
A2/C♯
44
love and strength for each new day, He will make a way.
D
A/C♯
F♯m7(4)
Bm7
mp
46
rit.
He will make a way.
Dmaj7/E
E
A2
rit.

He Is Able

**Words and Music by
RORY NOLAND and
GREG FERGUSON**

© Copyright 1989 Maranatha Praise, Inc. (administered by The Copyright Company, 40 Music Square East, Nashville, TN 37203).
All rights reserved. International copyright secured. Used by permission. CCLI# 115420

Holy and Anointed One

Words and Music by
JOHN BARNETT

© Copyright 1988 Mercy/Vineyard Publishing c/o Music Services, 209 Chapelwood Drive, Franklin, TN 37064.
All rights reserved. International copyright secured. Used by permission. CCLI# 164361

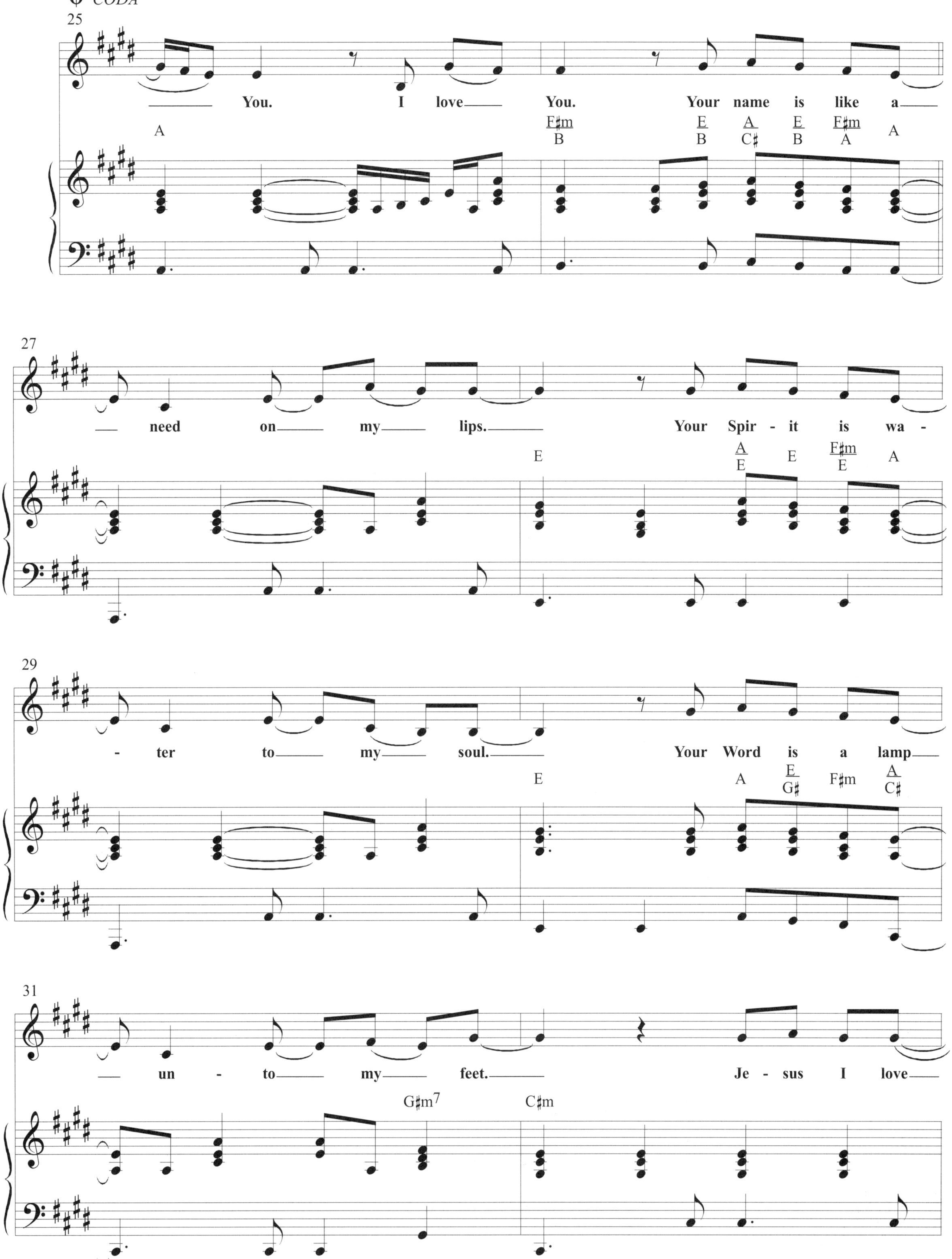
CODA
25
You. I love You. Your name is like a
A F♯m/B E/B A/C♯ E/B F♯m/A A
27
need on my lips. Your Spir - it is wa -
E A/E E F♯m/E A
29
- ter to my soul. Your Word is a lamp
E A E/G♯ F♯m A/C♯
31
un - to my feet. Je - sus I love
G♯m7 C♯m

Holy Ground

**Words and Music by
GERON DAVIS**

© Copyright 1983 Meadowgreen Music Company/Songchannel Music Group.
All rights administered by EMI Christian Music Publishing, 101 Winners Circle, P.O. Box 5085, Brentwood, TN 37024-5085.
All rights reserved. International copyright secured. Used by permission. CCLI# 21198

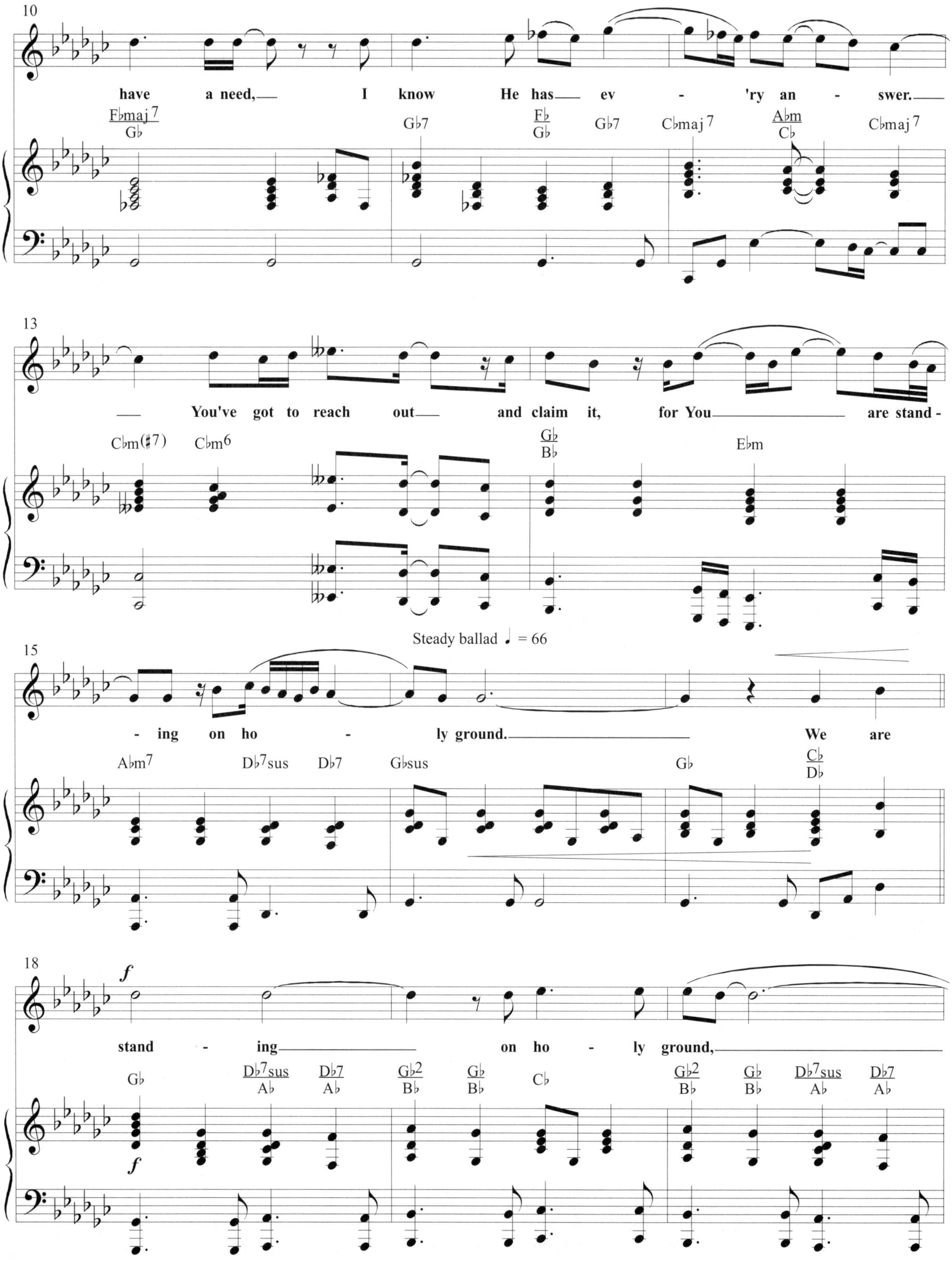
10
have a need, I know He has ev - 'ry an - swer.
F♭maj7/G♭ G♭7 F♭/G♭ G♭7 C♭maj7 A♭m/C♭ C♭maj7
13
You've got to reach out and claim it, for You are stand -
C♭m(♯7) C♭m6 G♭/B♭ E♭m
15
Steady ballad ♩ = 66
- ing on ho - ly ground. We are
A♭m7 D♭7sus D♭7 G♭sus G♭ C♭/D♭
18
f
stand - ing on ho - ly ground,
G♭ D♭7sus/A♭ D♭7/A♭ G♭2/B♭ G♭/B♭ C♭ G♭2/B♭ G♭/B♭ D♭7sus/A♭ D♭7/A♭

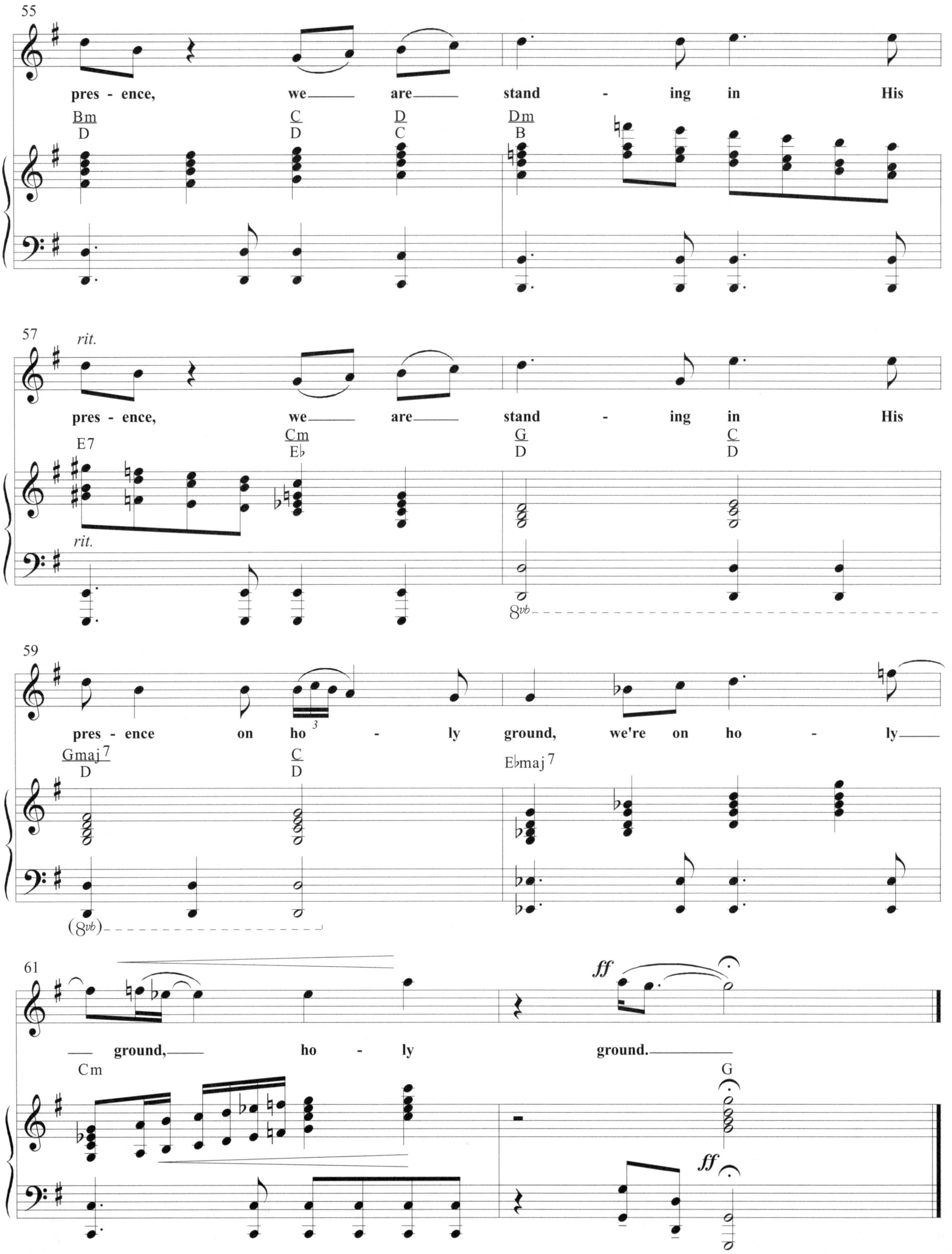
55
pres - ence, we are stand - ing in His
Bm/D C/D D/C Dm/B
57
rit.
pres - ence, we are stand - ing in His
E7 Cm/E♭ G/D C/D
rit.
8vb
59
pres - ence on ho - ly ground, we're on ho - ly
Gmaj7/D C/D E♭maj7
(8vb)
61
ground, ho - ly ground.
ff
Cm G
ff

Hungry (Falling on My Knees)

**Words and Music by
KATHRYN SCOTT**

© Copyright 1999 Vineyard Songs (UK/EIRE) Administered by Mercy/Vineyard Publishing in North America
c/o Music Services, 209 Chapelwood Drive, Franklin, TN 37064.
All rights reserved. International copyright secured. Used by permission. CCLI# 2650364

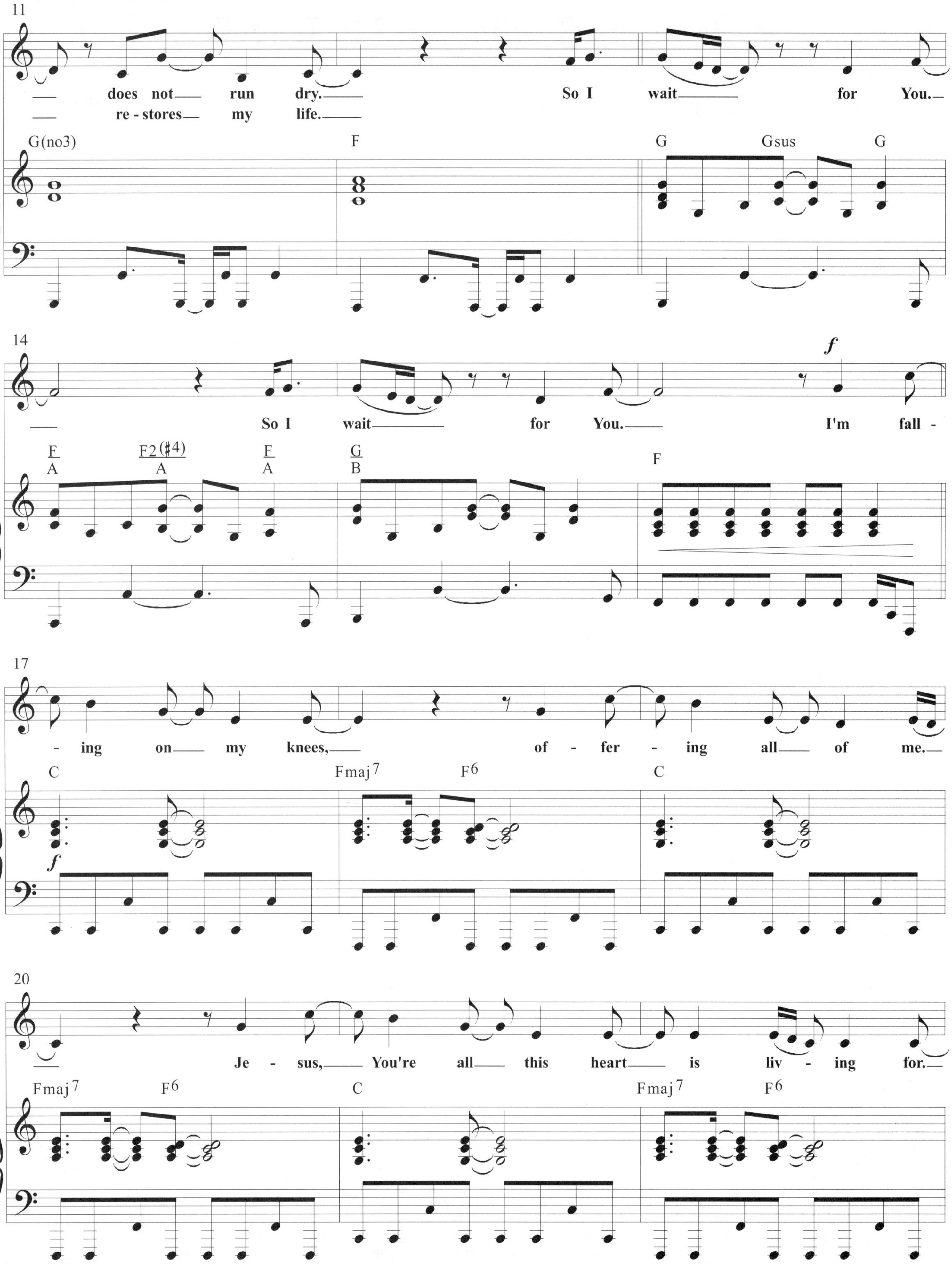
11
does not run dry. So I wait for You.
re - stores my life.
G(no3)
F
G
Gsus
G
14
So I wait for You. I'm fall -
F/A
F2(♯4)/A
F/A
G/B
F
f
17
- ing on my knees, of - fer - ing all of me.
C
Fmaj7
F6
C
f
20
Je - sus, You're all this heart is liv - ing for.
Fmaj7
F6
C
Fmaj7
F6

I Believe in Jesus

Words and Music by
MARC NELSON

© Copyright 1987 Mercy/Vineyard Publishing c/o Music Services, 209 Chapelwood Drive, Franklin, TN 37064.
All rights reserved. International copyright secured. Used by permission. CCLI# 61282

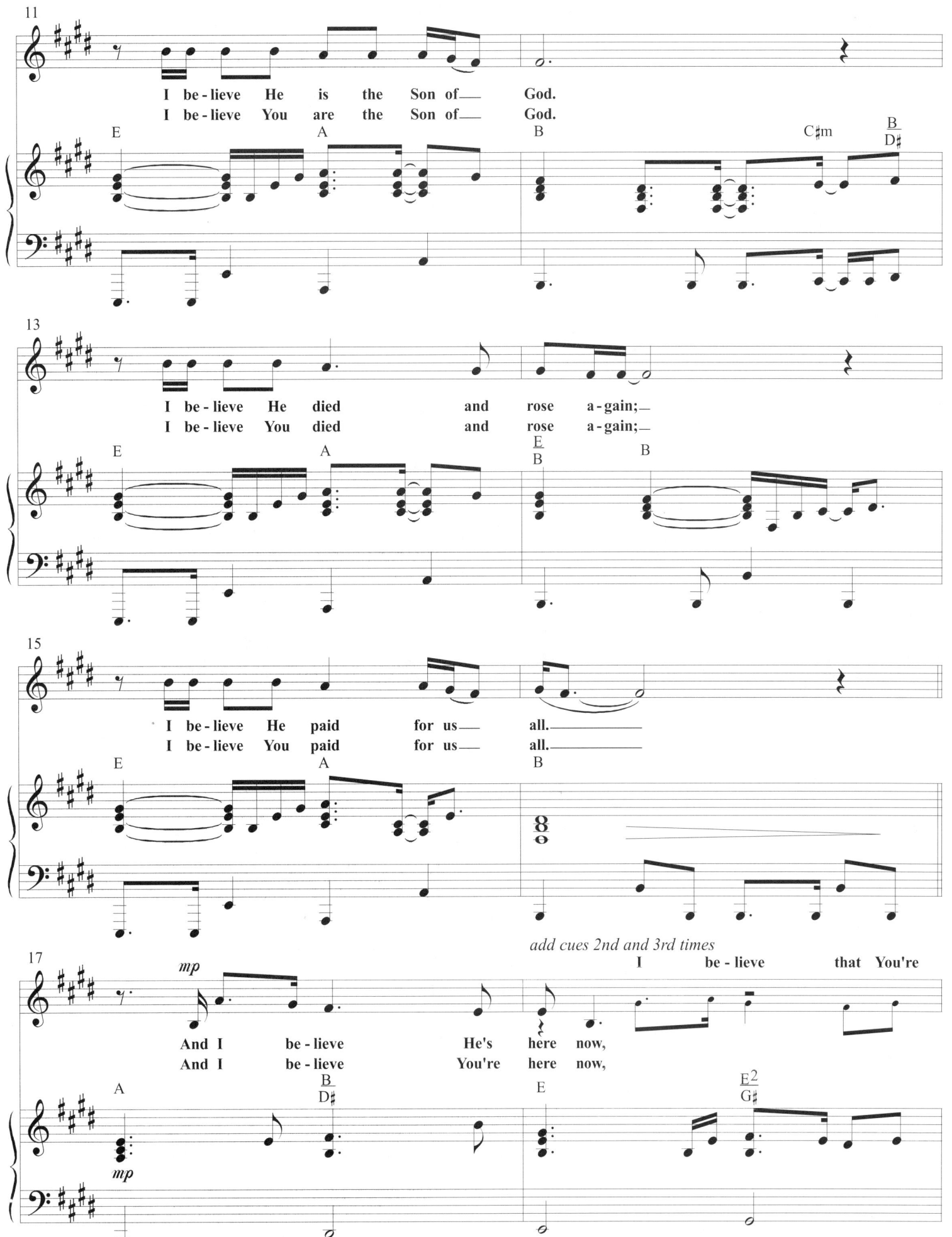

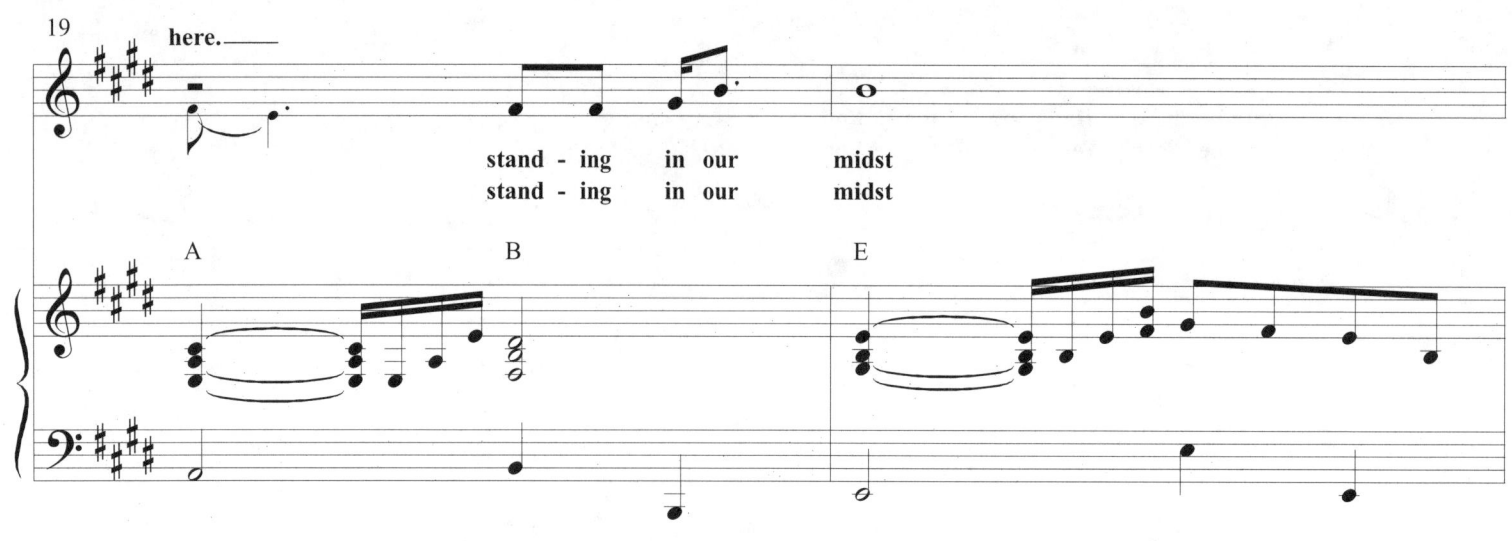
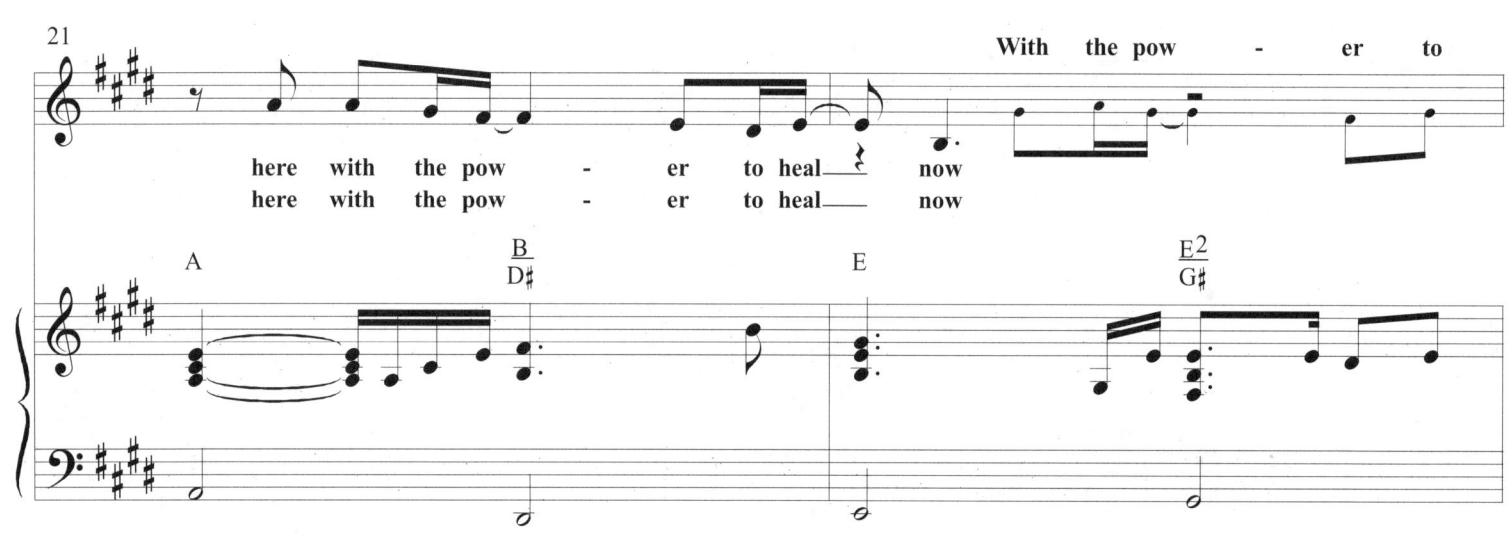

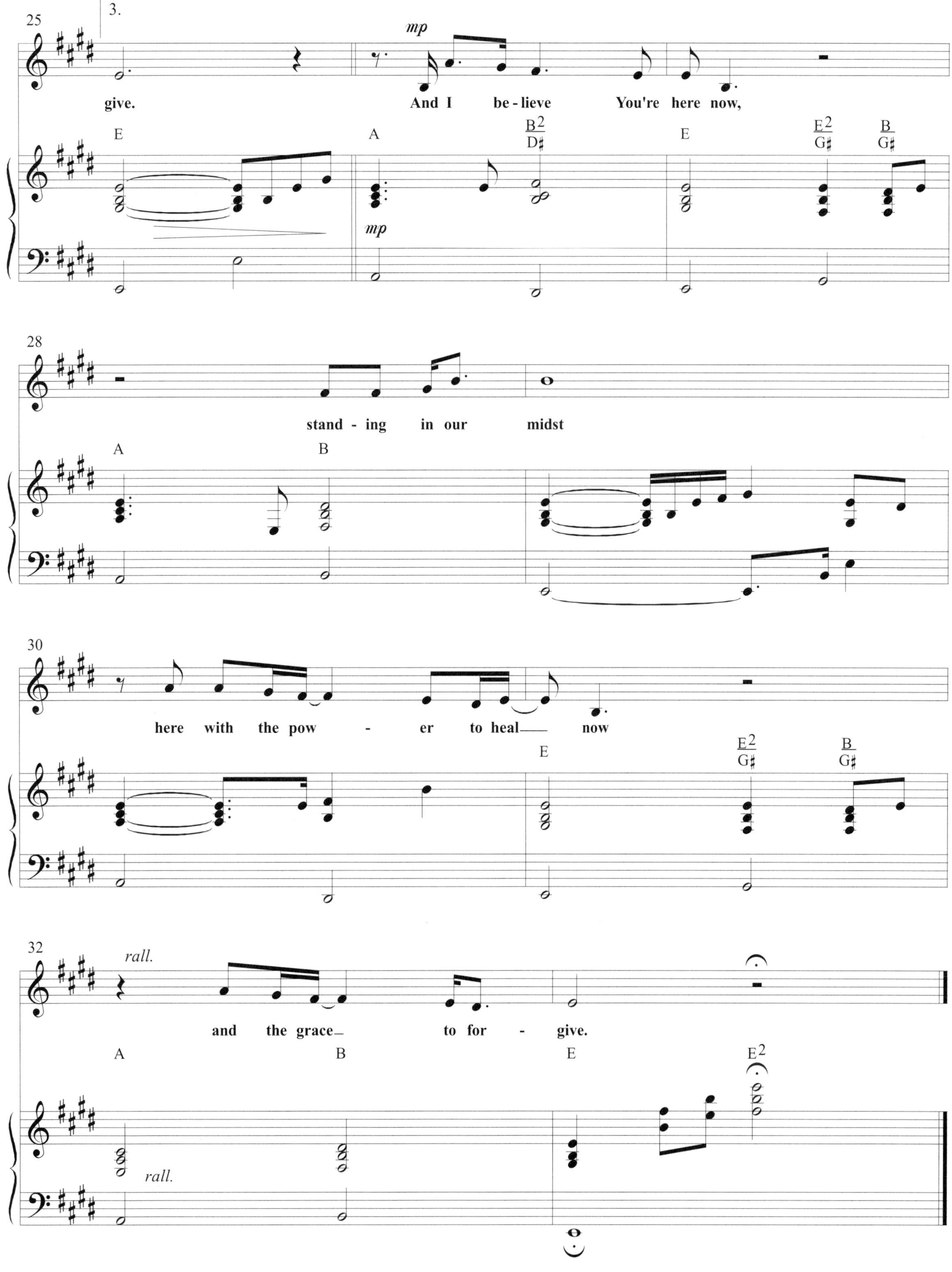
25
3.
mp
give. And I be-lieve You're here now,
E A B2/D♯ E E2/G♯ B/G♯
mp
28
stand - ing in our midst
A B
30
here with the pow - er to heal___ now
E E2/G♯ B/G♯
32
rall.
and the grace___ to for - give.
A B E E2
rall.

I See the Lord

**Words and Music by
CHRIS FALSON**

Worshipfully ♩ = 76-80

mp

I see the Lord___ seat-ed on___ the throne___ ex-alt-ed,___ and the train of His robe___ fills the tem-ple with glo-

© Copyright 1993 Maranatha Praise, Inc. (administered by The Copyright Company, 40 Music Square East, Nashville, TN 37203).
All rights reserved. International copyright secured. Used by permission. CCLI# 1406176

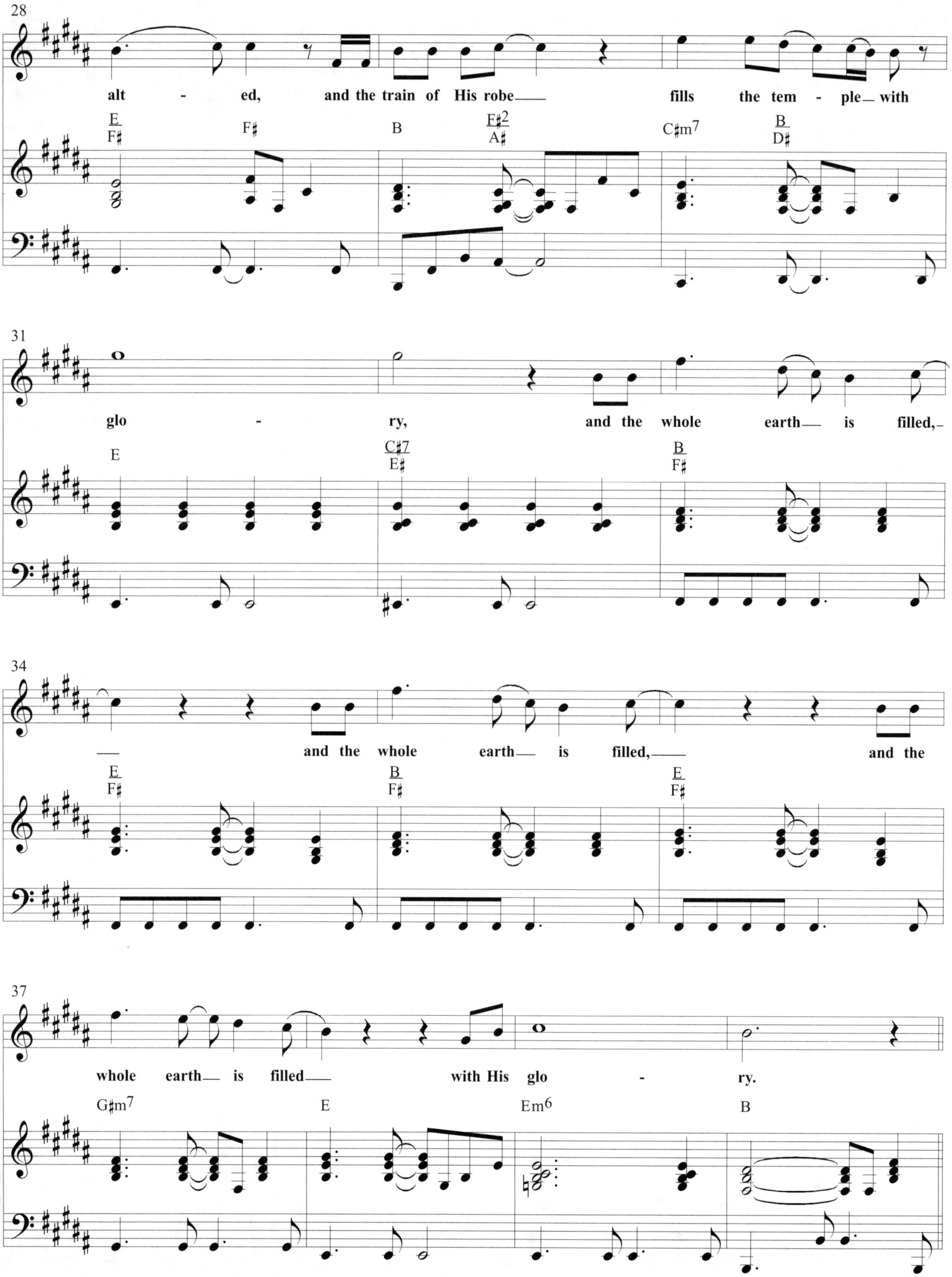
28
alt - ed, and the train of His robe___ fills the tem - ple—with
E/F♯ F♯ B F♯2/A♯ C♯m7 B/D♯
31
glo - ry, and the whole earth___ is filled,—
E C♯7/E♯ B/F♯
34
— and the whole earth___ is filled,___ and the
E/F♯ B/F♯ E/F♯
37
whole earth___ is filled___ with His glo - ry.
G♯m7 E Em6 B

I Walk by Faith

Words and Music by
CHRIS FALSON

© Copyright 1990 Maranatha Praise, Inc. (administered by The Copyright Company, 40 Music Square East, Nashville, TN 37203).
All rights reserved. International copyright secured. Used by permission. CCLI# 464834

I Will Celebrate

**Words and Music by
RITA BALOCHE**

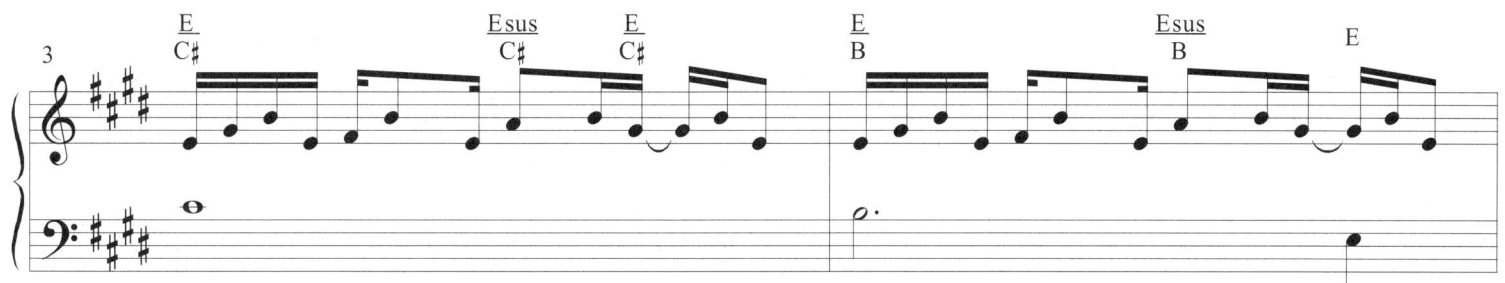
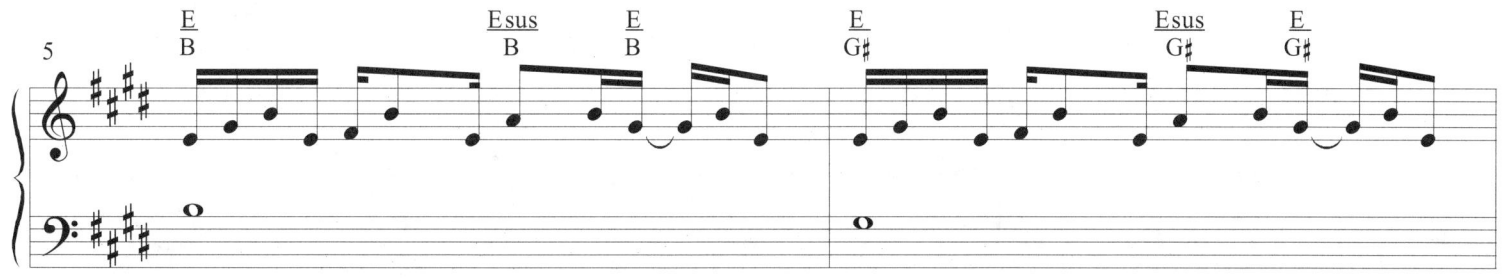
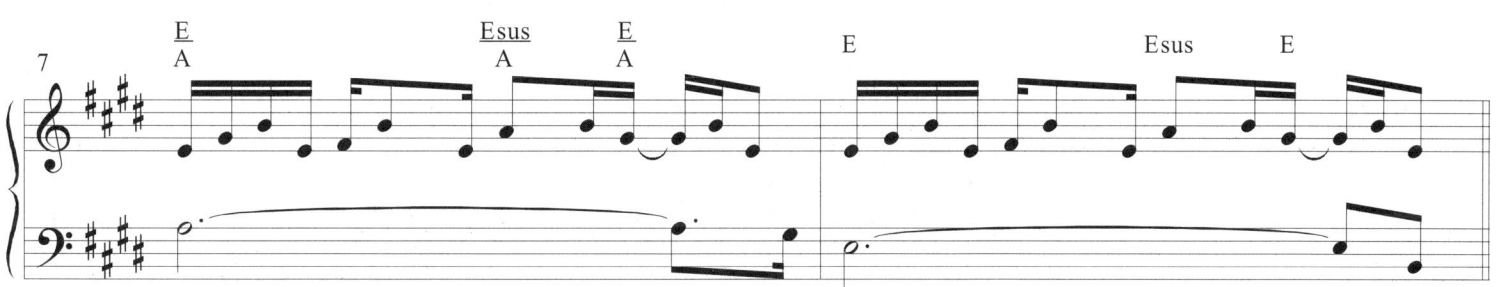

© Copyright 1990 Maranatha Praise, Inc. (administered by The Copyright Company, 40 Music Square East, Nashville, TN 37203).
All rights reserved. International copyright secured. Used by permission. CCLI# 443123

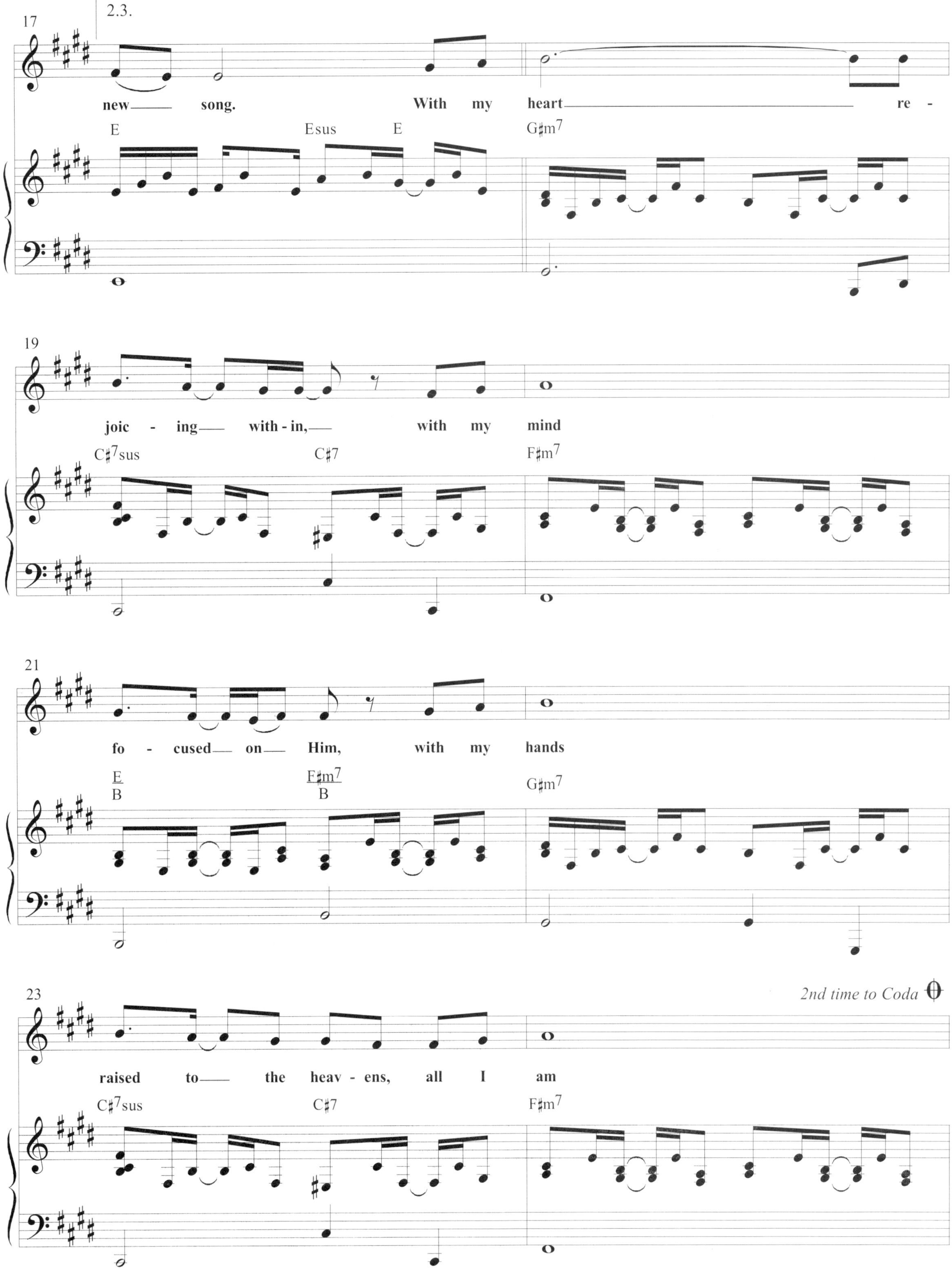
17
2.3.
new song. With my heart re -
E Esus E G♯m7
19
joic - ing within, with my mind
C♯7sus C♯7 F♯m7
21
fo - cused on Him, with my hands
E/B F♯m7/B G♯m7
23
2nd time to Coda
raised to the heav - ens, all I am
C♯7sus C♯7 F♯m7

I Will Not Forget You

Words and Music by
BEN and ROBIN PASLEY

© Copyright 1999 Corinthian Music (administered by The Copyright Company, 40 Music Square East, Nashville, TN 37203).
All rights reserved. International copyright secured. Used by permission. CCLI# 2694306

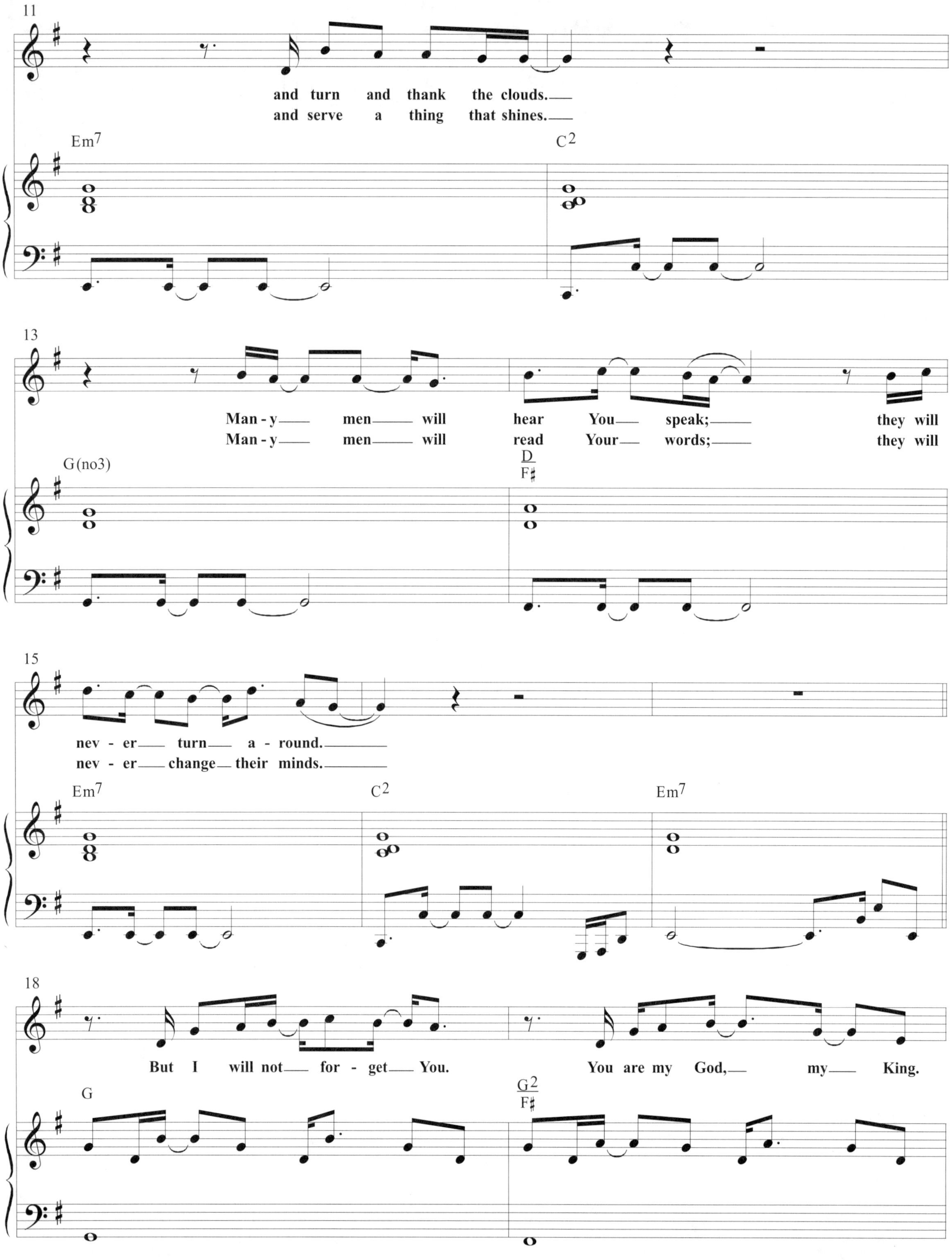

and turn and thank the clouds.
and serve a thing that shines.

Man-y men will hear You speak; they will
Man-y men will read Your words; they will

nev-er turn a-round.
nev-er change their minds.

But I will not for-get You. You are my God, my King.

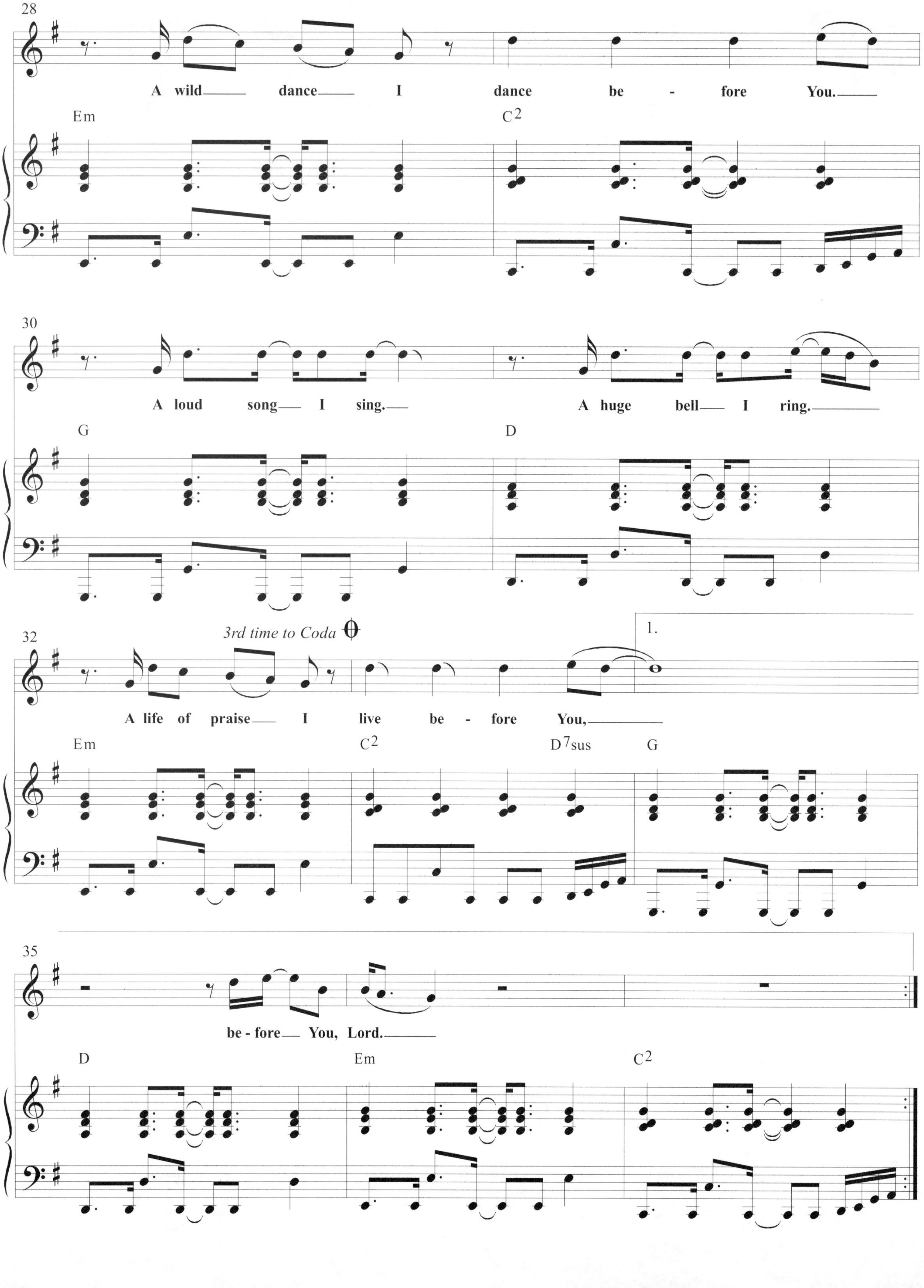
28
A wild dance I dance be - fore You.
Em
C2
30
A loud song I sing.
A huge bell I ring.
G
D
32
3rd time to Coda
A life of praise I live be - fore You,
1.
Em
C2
D7sus
G
35
be - fore You, Lord.
D
Em
C2

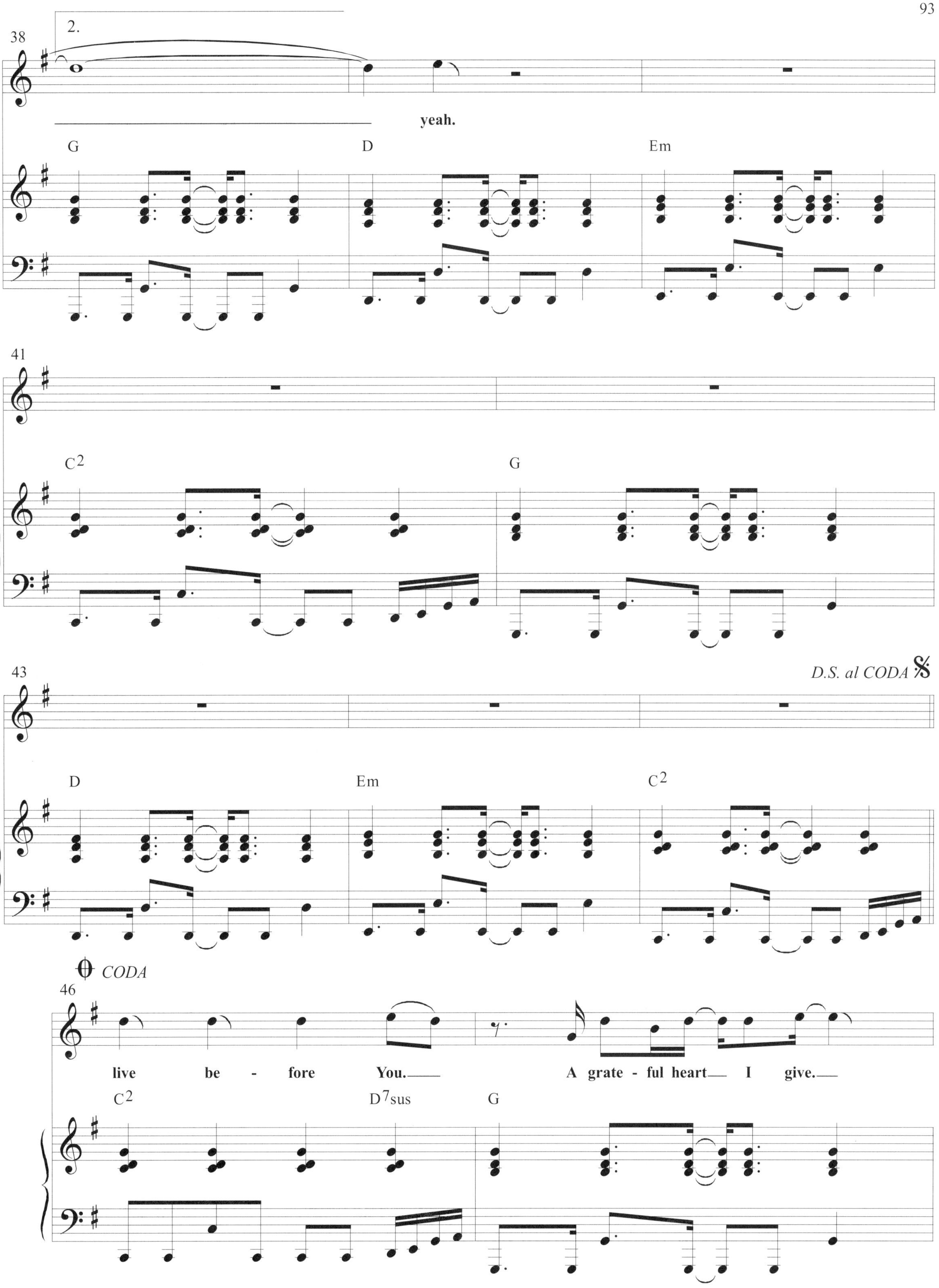
38
2.
yeah.
G
D
Em
41
C2
G
43
D.S. al CODA
D
Em
C2
CODA
46
live be - fore You.
A grate - ful heart I give.
C2
D7sus
G

In That Day

Words and Music by
JOSEPH SABOLICK

© Copyright 1999 Maranatha! Music (administered by The Copyright Company, 40 Music Square East, Nashville, TN 37203).
All rights reserved. International copyright secured. Used by permission. CCLI# 2753601

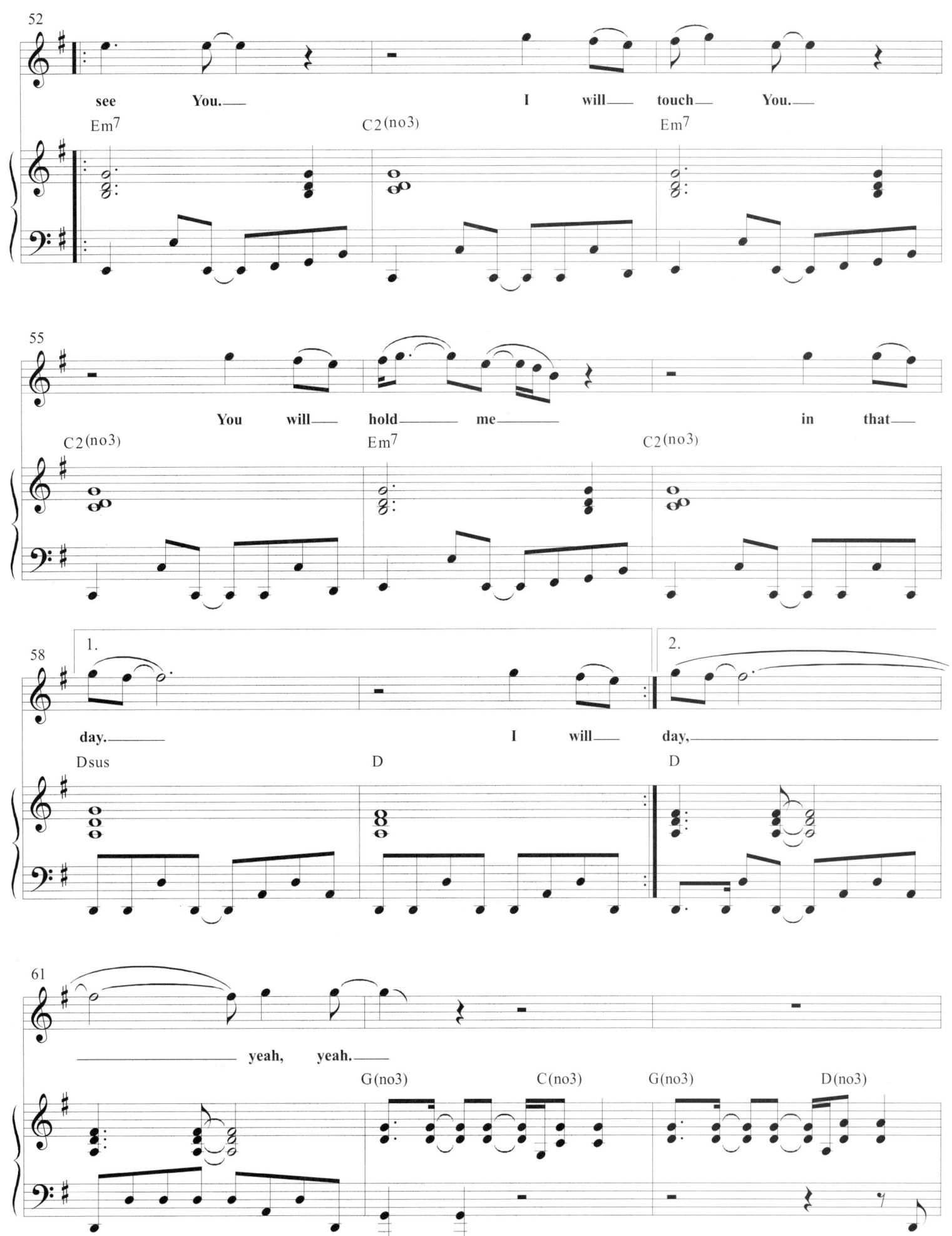

In the Secret

**Words and Music by
ANDY PARK**

© Copyright 1995 Mercy/Vineyard Publishing c/o Music Services, 209 Chapelwood Drive, Franklin, TN 37064.
All rights reserved. International copyright secured. Used by permission. CCLI# 1810119

Jesus Is Alive

**Words and Music by
RON KENOLY**

© Copyright 1987 Integrity's Hosanna! Music c/o Integrity Music, Inc., 1000 Cody Road, Mobile, AL 36695.
All rights reserved. International copyright secured. Used by permission. CCLI# 550652

Jesus, Lover of My Soul

Words and Music by
JOHN EZZY, DANIEL GRUL, and
STEPHEN McPHERSON

© Copyright 1992 John Ezzy/Daniel Grul/Stephen McPherson/Hillsongs Publishing
(administered in the U.S. and Canada by Integrity's Hosanna! Music) c/o Integrity Music, Inc., 1000 Cody Road, Mobile, AL 36695.
All rights reserved. International copyright secured. Used by permission. CCLI# 1198817

Light the Fire Again

**Words and Music by
BRAIN DOERKSEN**

© Copyright 1994 Mercy/Vineyard Publishing c/o Music Services,
209 Chapelwood Drive, Franklin, TN 37064.
All rights reserved. International copyright secured. Used by permission. CCLI# 1346920

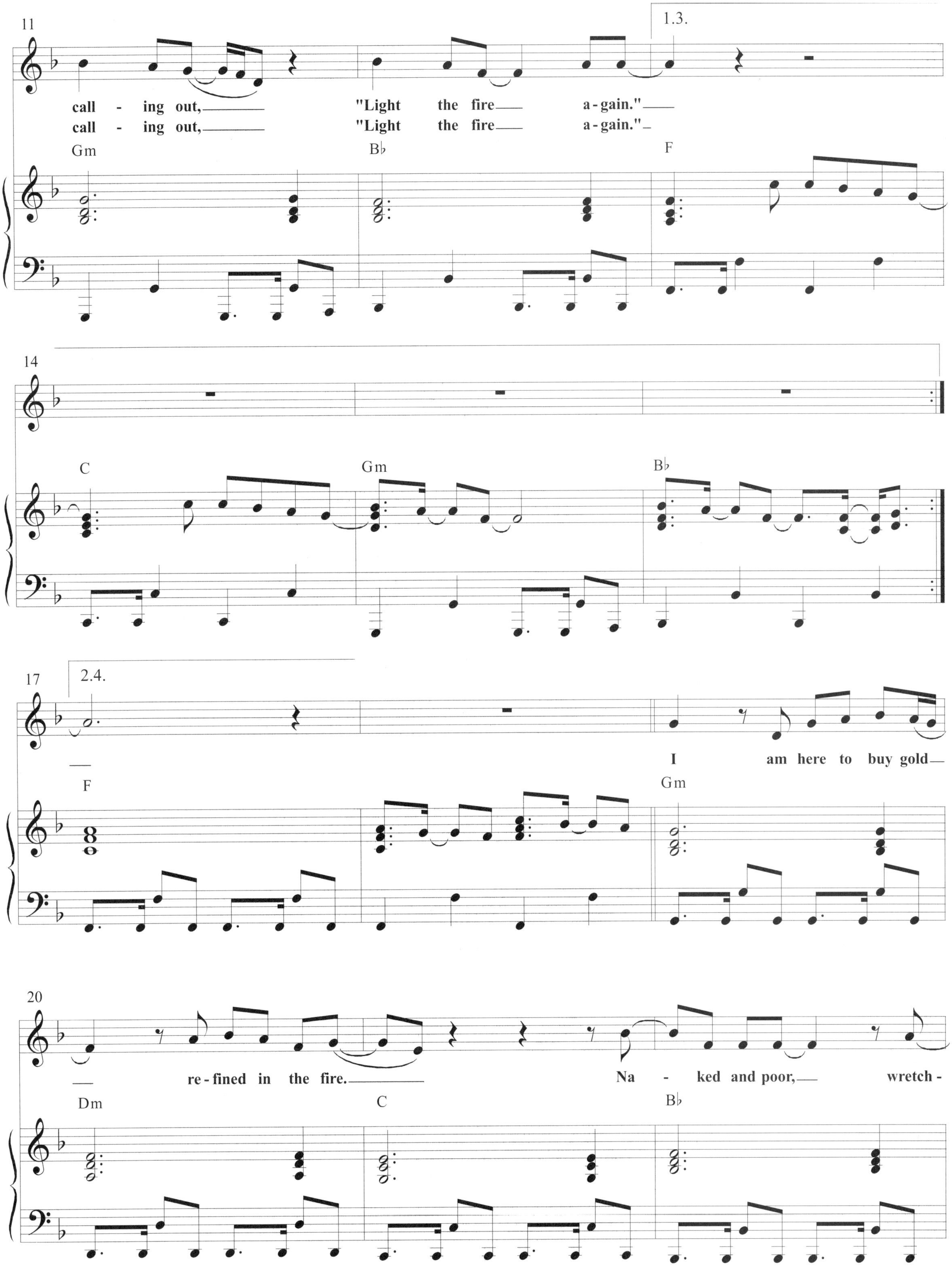
11
1.3.
call - ing out, "Light the fire a - gain."
call - ing out, "Light the fire a - gain."
Gm
B♭
F
14
C
Gm
B♭
17
2.4.
I am here to buy gold
F
Gm
20
re - fined in the fire. Na - ked and poor, wretch -
Dm
C
B♭

-ed and blind I come. Clothe me in white so I won't be a-shamed. Lord, light the fire a-gain.

Ah, oh, light the fire a-gain.

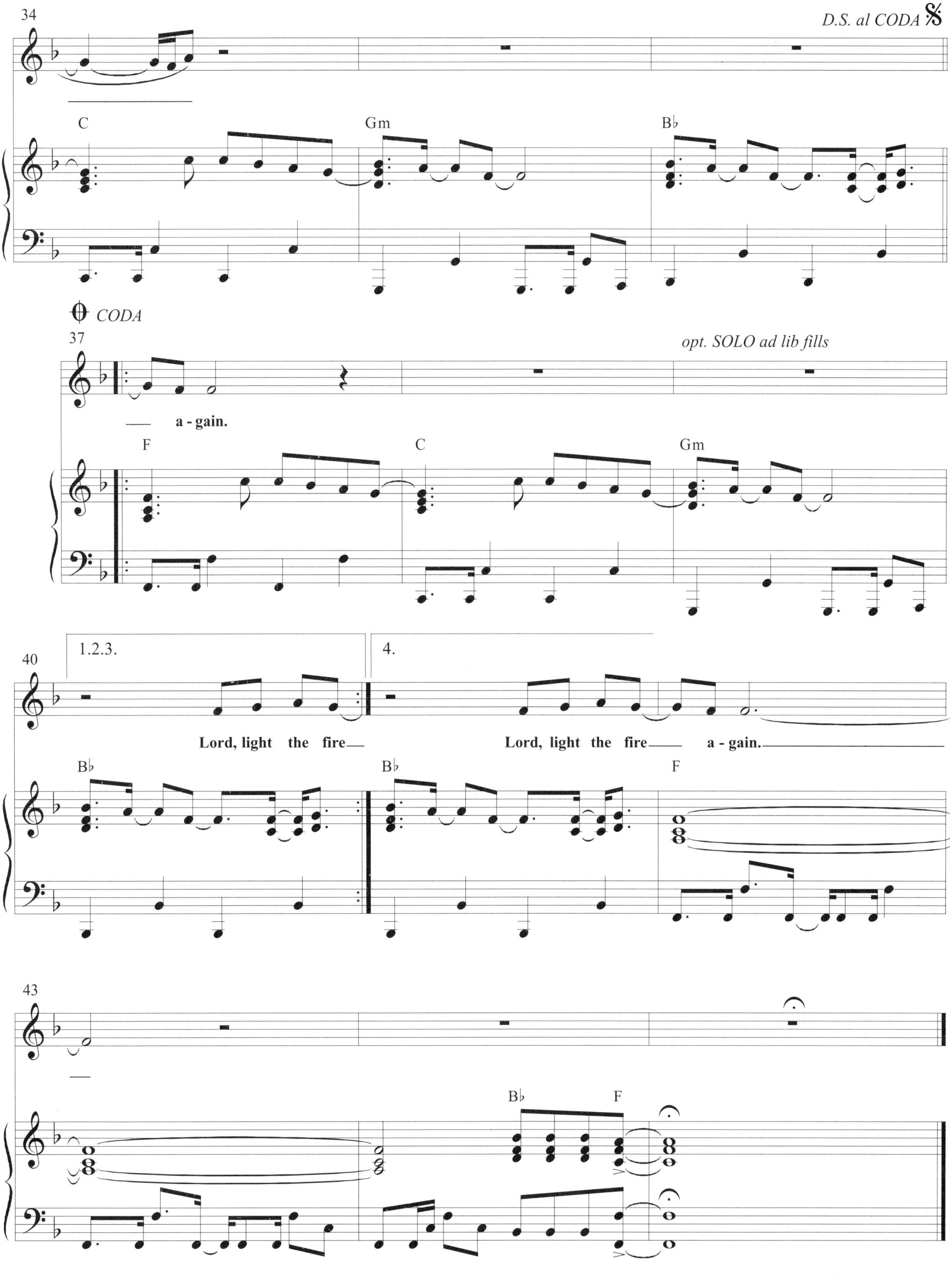
34
D.S. al CODA
C
Gm
B♭
CODA
37
opt. SOLO ad lib fills
a - gain.
F
C
Gm
40
1.2.3.
4.
Lord, light the fire
Lord, light the fire a - gain.
B♭
B♭
F
43
B♭
F

Redeemer, Savior, Friend

**Words and Music by
DARRELL EVANS and
CHRIS SPRINGER**

© Copyright 1999 Integrity's Hosanna! Music and Integrity's Praise! Music c/o Integrity Music, Inc., 1000 Cody Road, Mobile, AL 36695.
All rights reserved. International copyright secured. Used by permission. CCLI# 2831523

Rock of Ages

Words and Music by
RITA BALOCHE

© Copyright 1997 Maranatha Praise, Inc. (administered by The Copyright Company, 40 Music Square East, Nashville, TN 37203).
All rights reserved. International copyright secured. Used by permission. CCLI# 2240547

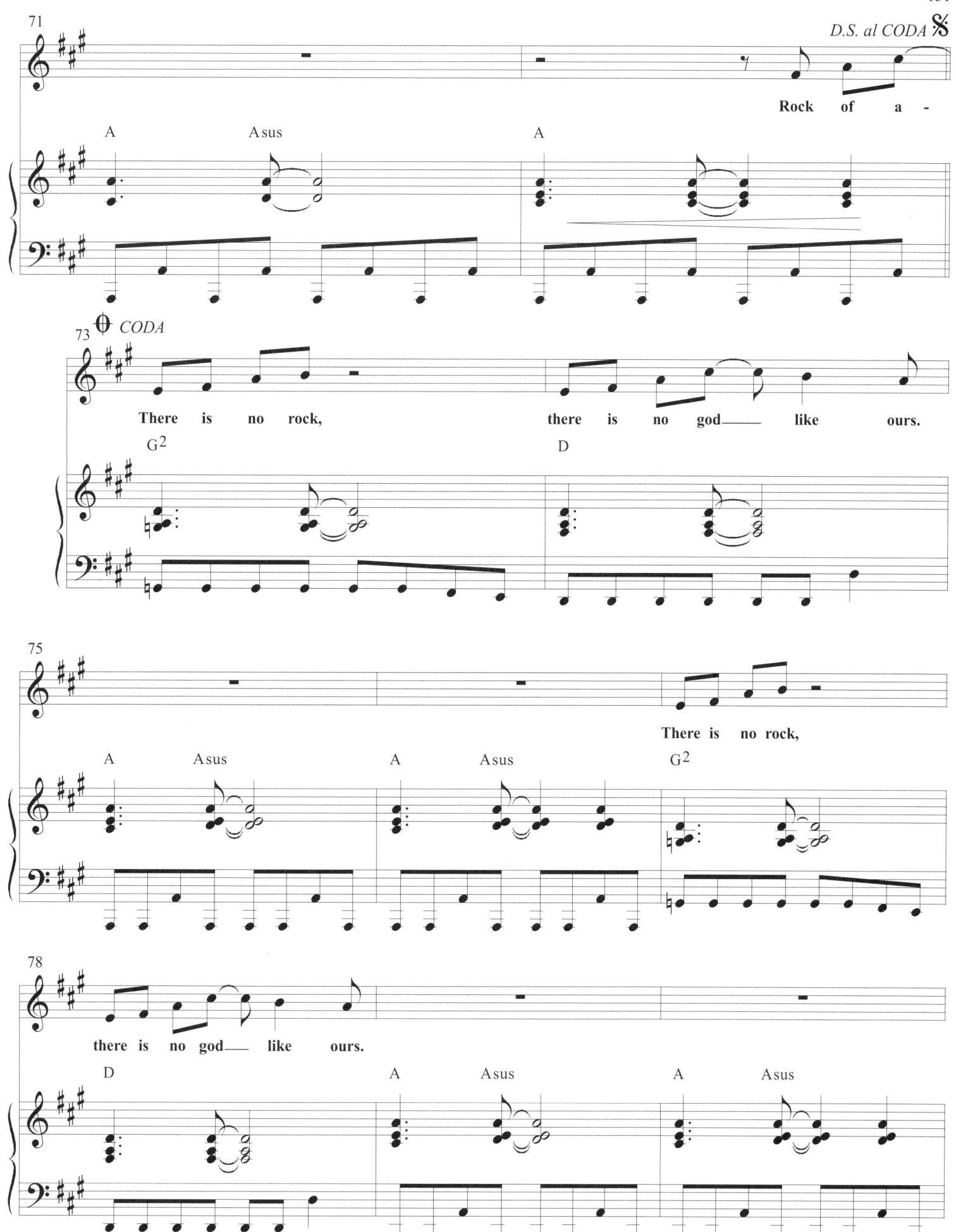

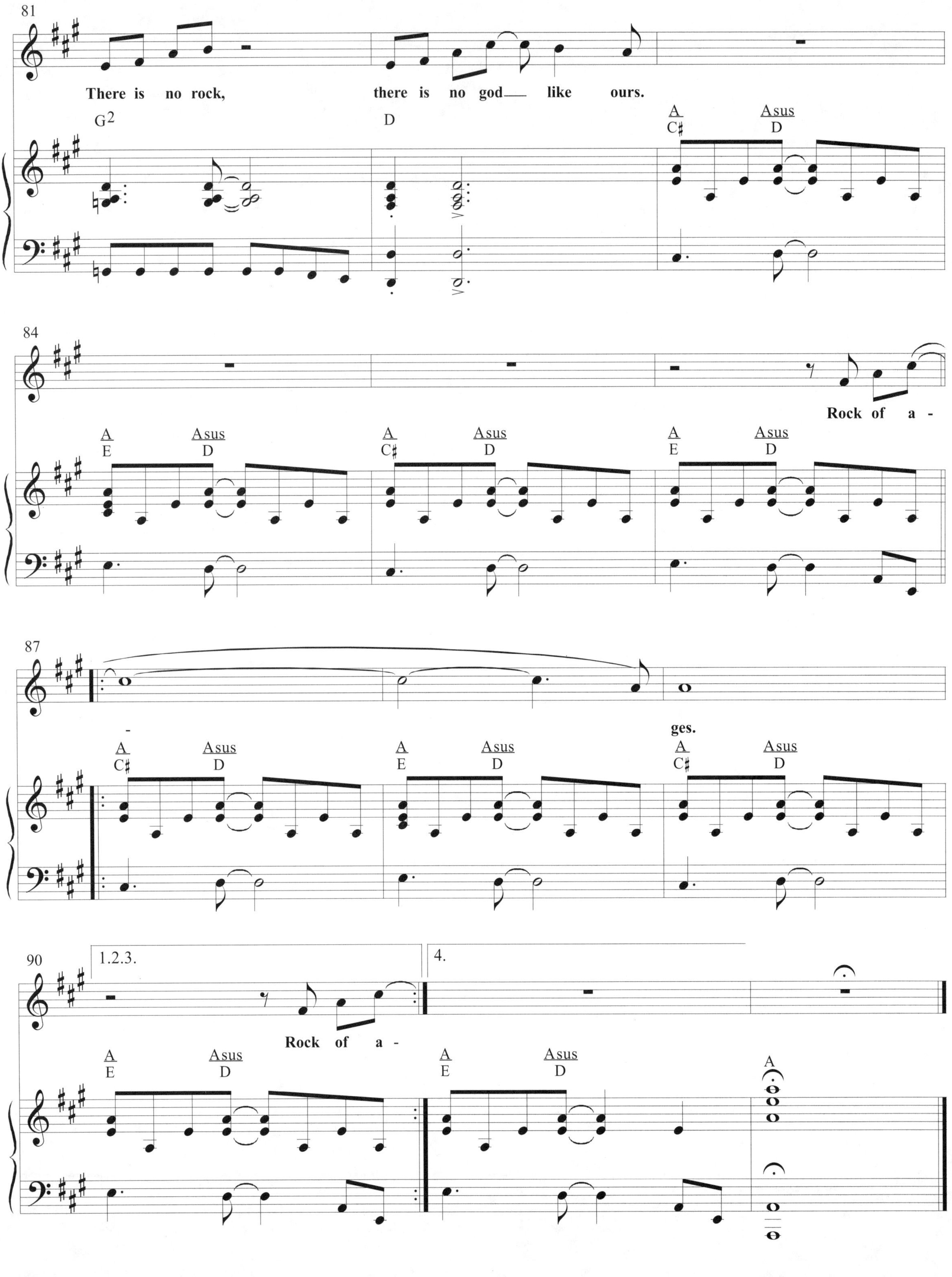
81
There is no rock, there is no god like ours.
G2
D
A/C♯ Asus/D
84
Rock of a -
A/E Asus/D
A/C♯ Asus/D
A/E Asus/D
87
- ges.
A/C♯ Asus/D
A/E Asus/D
A/C♯ Asus/D
90
1.2.3.
4.
Rock of a -
A/E Asus/D
A/E Asus/D
A

Shine, Jesus, Shine

**Words and Music by
GRAHAM KENDRICK**

© Copyright 1987 Make Way Music c/o Music Services, 209 Chapelwood Drive, Franklin, TN 37064.
All rights reserved. International copyright secured. Used by permission. CCLI# 30426

There Is None Like You

Words and Music by LENNY LeBLANC

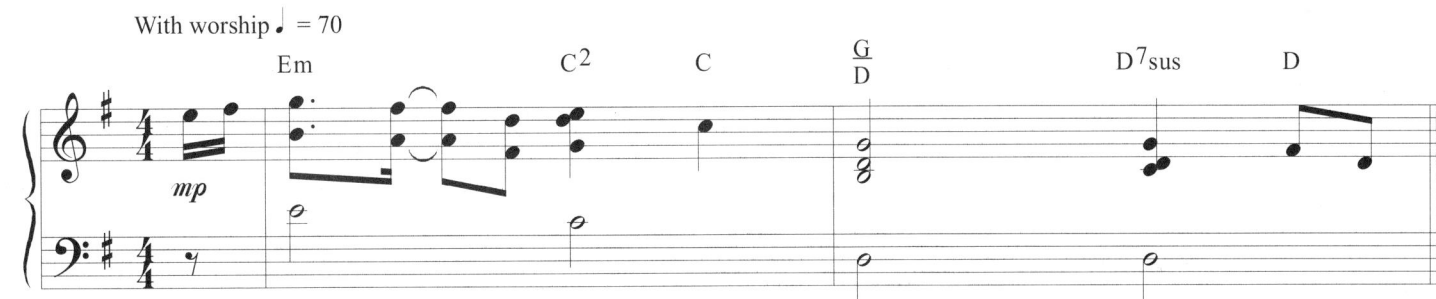

There is none like____ You.

No one else___ can touch___ my heart___ like You do.___

© Copyright 1991 Integrity's Hosanna! Music c/o Integrity Music, Inc., 1000 Cody Road, Mobile, AL 36695.
All rights reserved. International copyright secured. Used by permission. CCLI# 674545

Victory Chant

**Words and Music by
JOSEPH VOGELS**

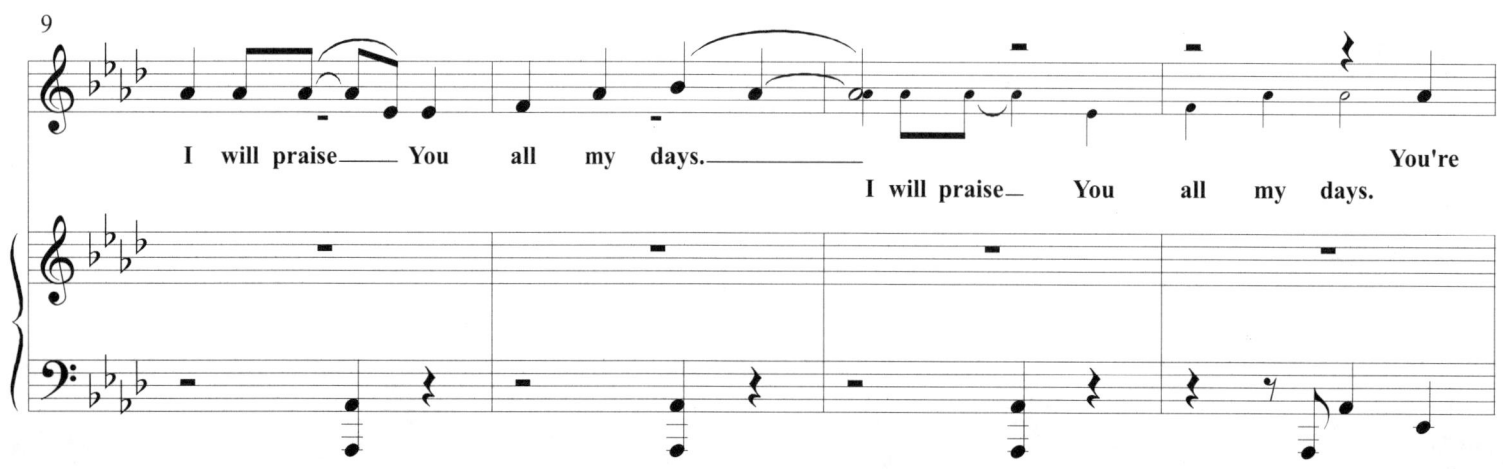

© Copyright 1985 Scripture In Song (a div. of Integrity Music, Inc.) c/o Integrity Music, 1000 Cody Road, AL 36695.
All rights reserved. International copyright secured. Used by permission. CCLI# 23873

We Want to See Jesus Lifted High

**Words and Music by
DOUG HORLEY**

© Copyright 1993 Kingsway's Thankyou Music. All rights in the Western Hemisphere administered in North America by EMI Christian Music Publishing, 101 Winners Circle, P.O. Box 5085, Brentwood, TN 37024-5085.
All rights reserved. International copyright secured. Used by permission. CCLI# 1033408

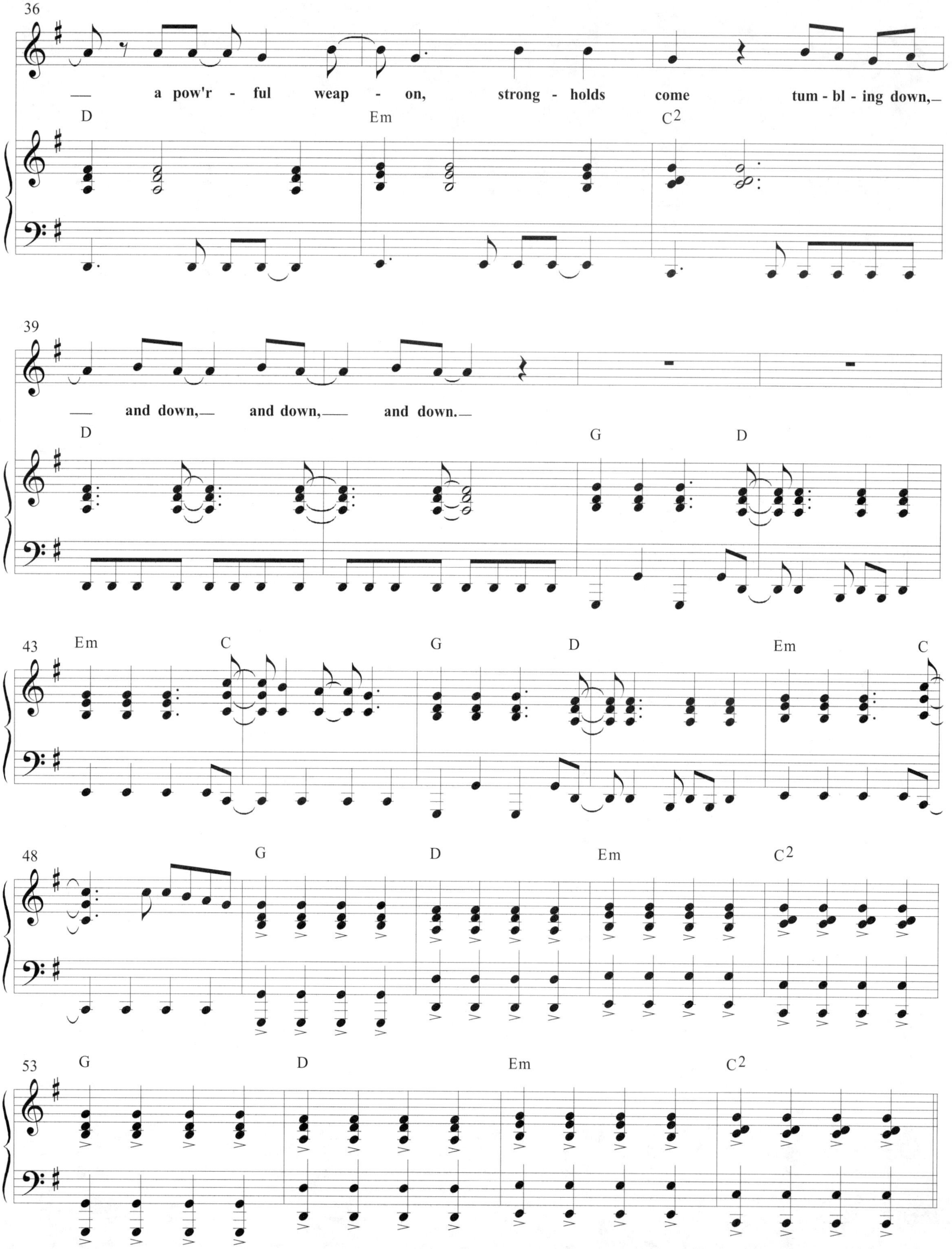
36
— a pow'r - ful weap - on, strong - holds come tum - bl - ing down,—
D Em C2
39
— and down,— and down,— and down.—
D G D
43
Em C G D Em C
48
G D Em C2
53
G D Em C2

We Will Dance

**Words and Music by
DAVID RUIS**

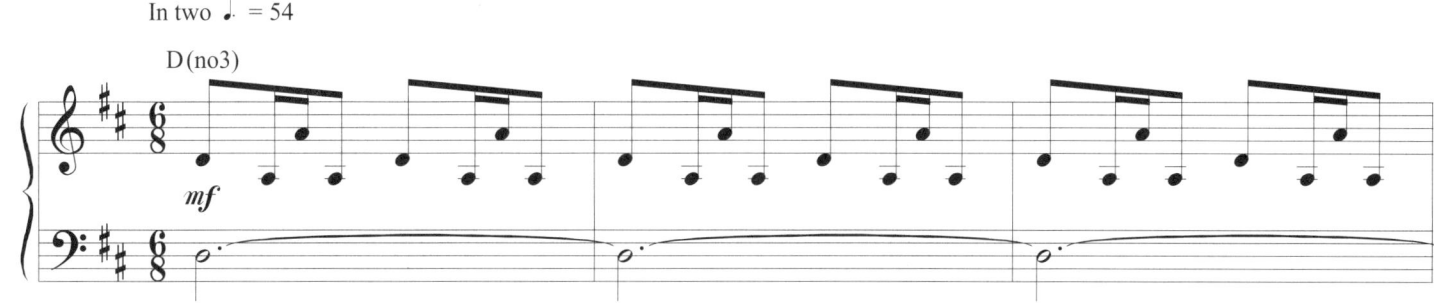
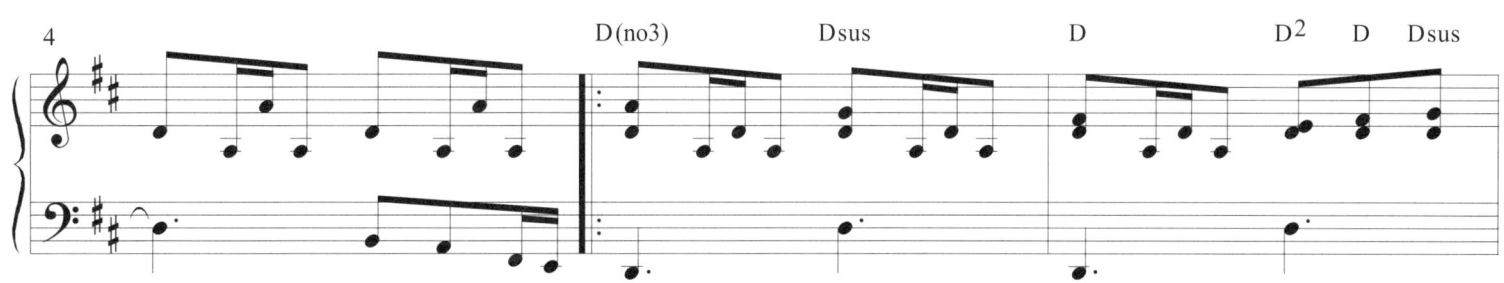
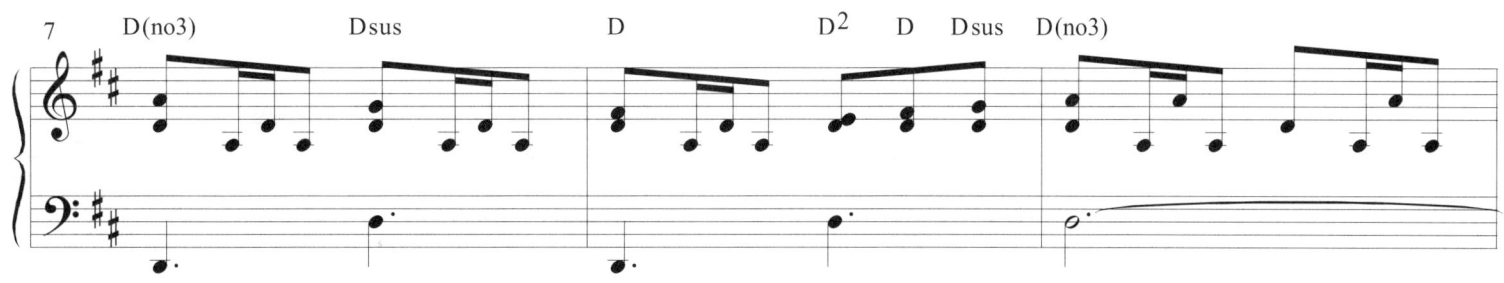

© Copyright 1993 Mercy/Vineyard Publishing c/o Music Services, 209 Chapelwood Drive, Franklin, TN 37064.
All rights reserved. International copyright secured. Used by permission. CCLI# 1034438

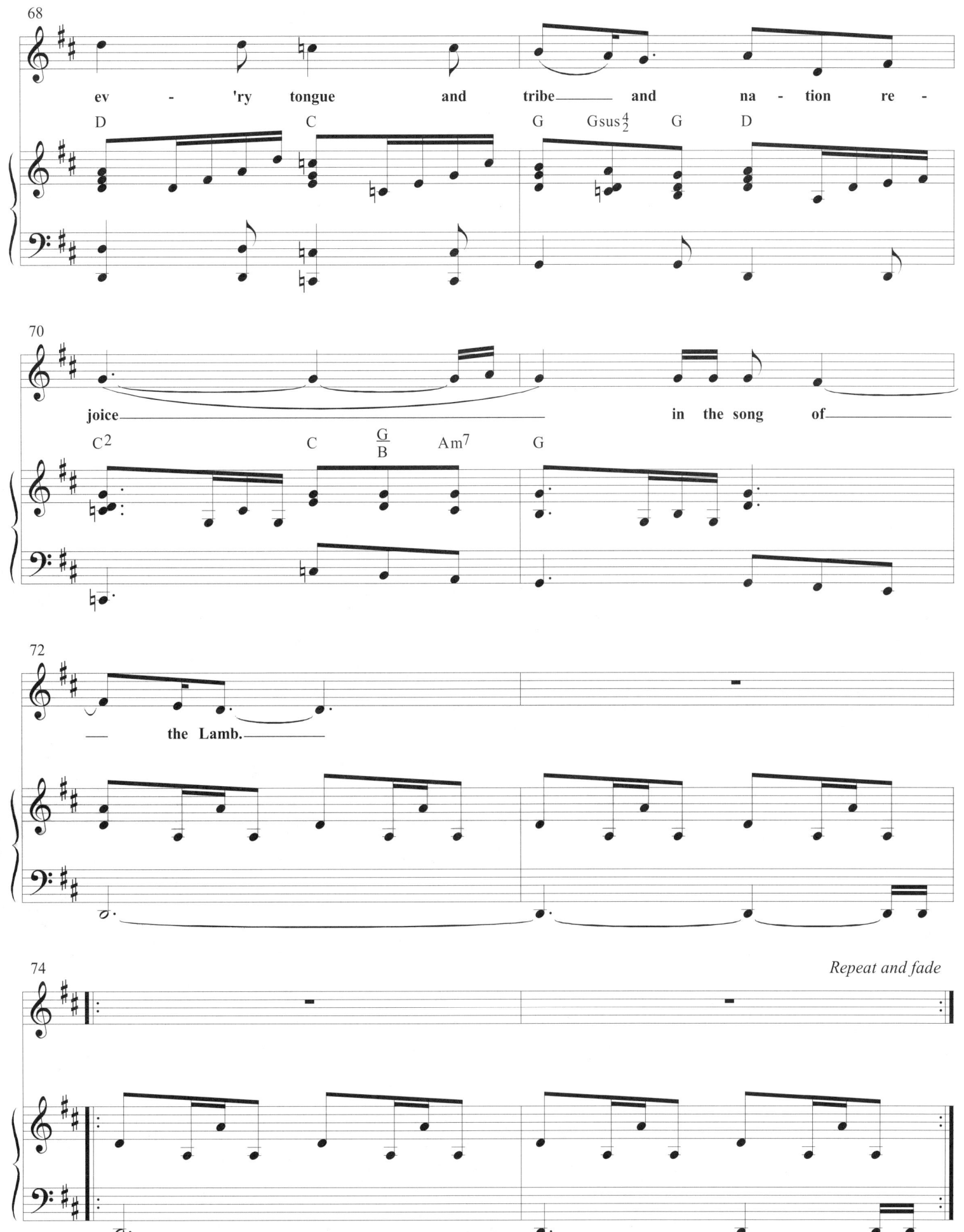

When I Look into Your Holiness

**Words and Music by
WAYNE and CATHY PERRIN**

© Copyright 1981 Integrity's Hosanna! Music c/o Integrity Music, Inc., 1000 Cody Road, Mobile, AL 36695.
All rights reserved. International copyright secured. Used by permission. CCLI# 16347

165

Worship You

**Words and Music by
JAMI SMITH**

With energy ♩ = 118

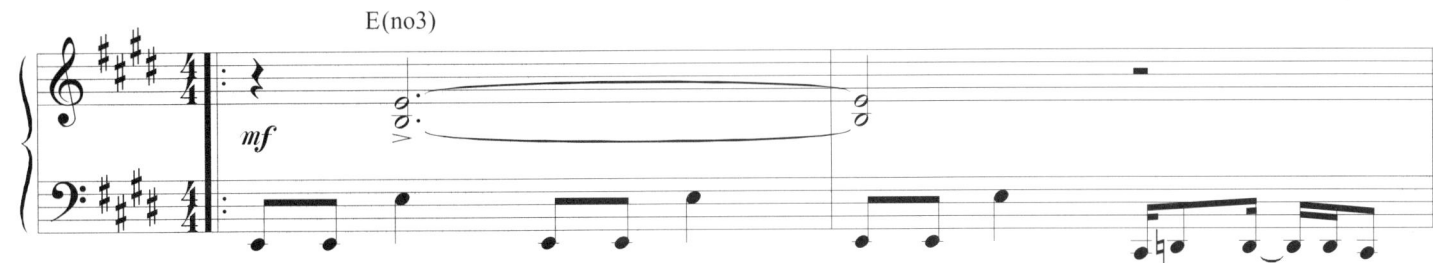

© Copyright 1998 Integrity's Hosanna! Music c/o Integrity Music, Inc., 1000 Cody Road, Mobile, AL 36695.
All rights reserved. International copyright secured. Used by permission.

You Are God

Words and Music by
SCOTT UNDERWOOD

© Copyright 1997 Mercy/Vineyard Publishing c/o Music Services, 209 Chapelwood Drive, Franklin, TN 37064.
All rights reserved. International copyright secured. Used by permission. CCLI# 2188427

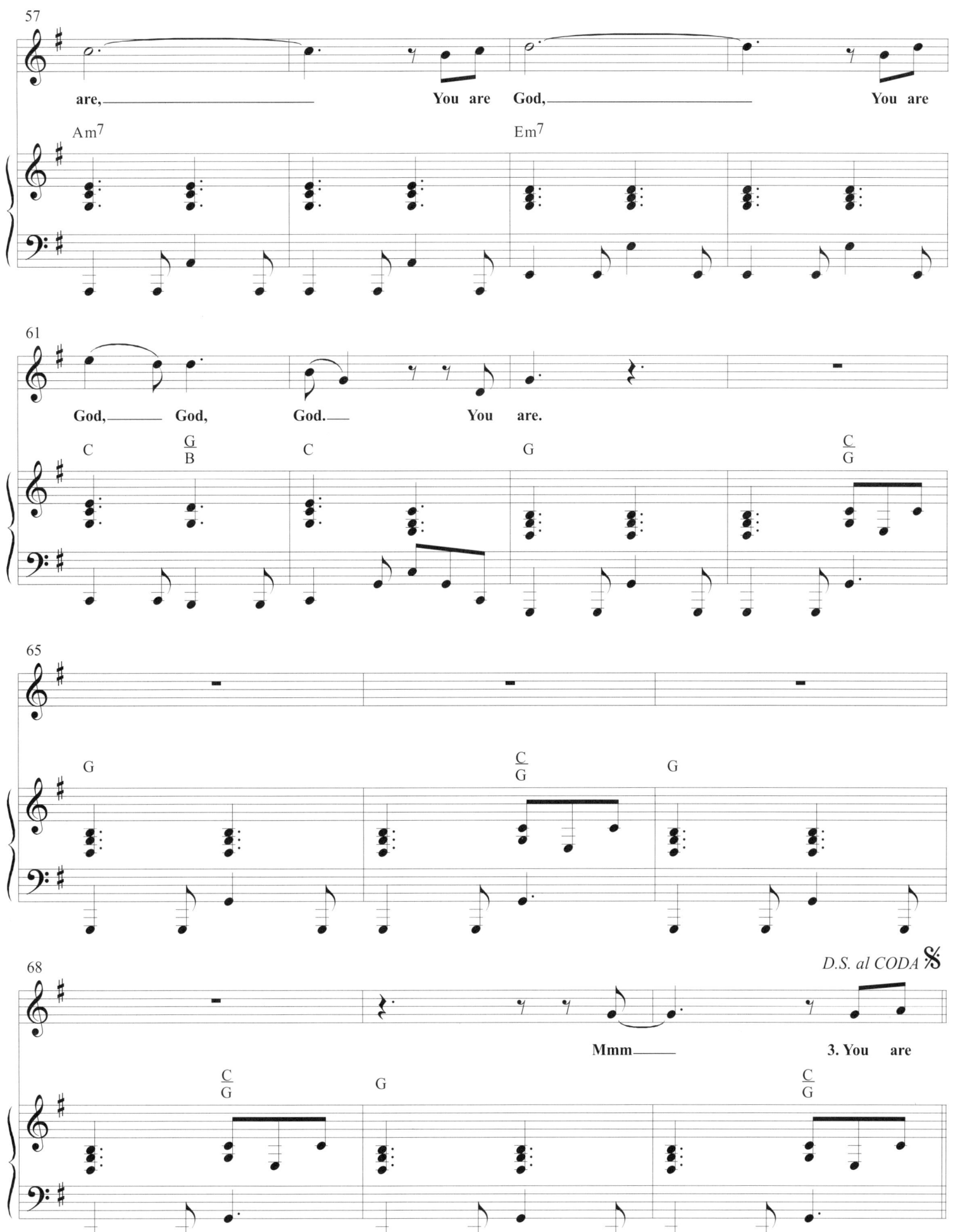